SPACE

HOW IT WORKS

SPACE

STUART CLARK

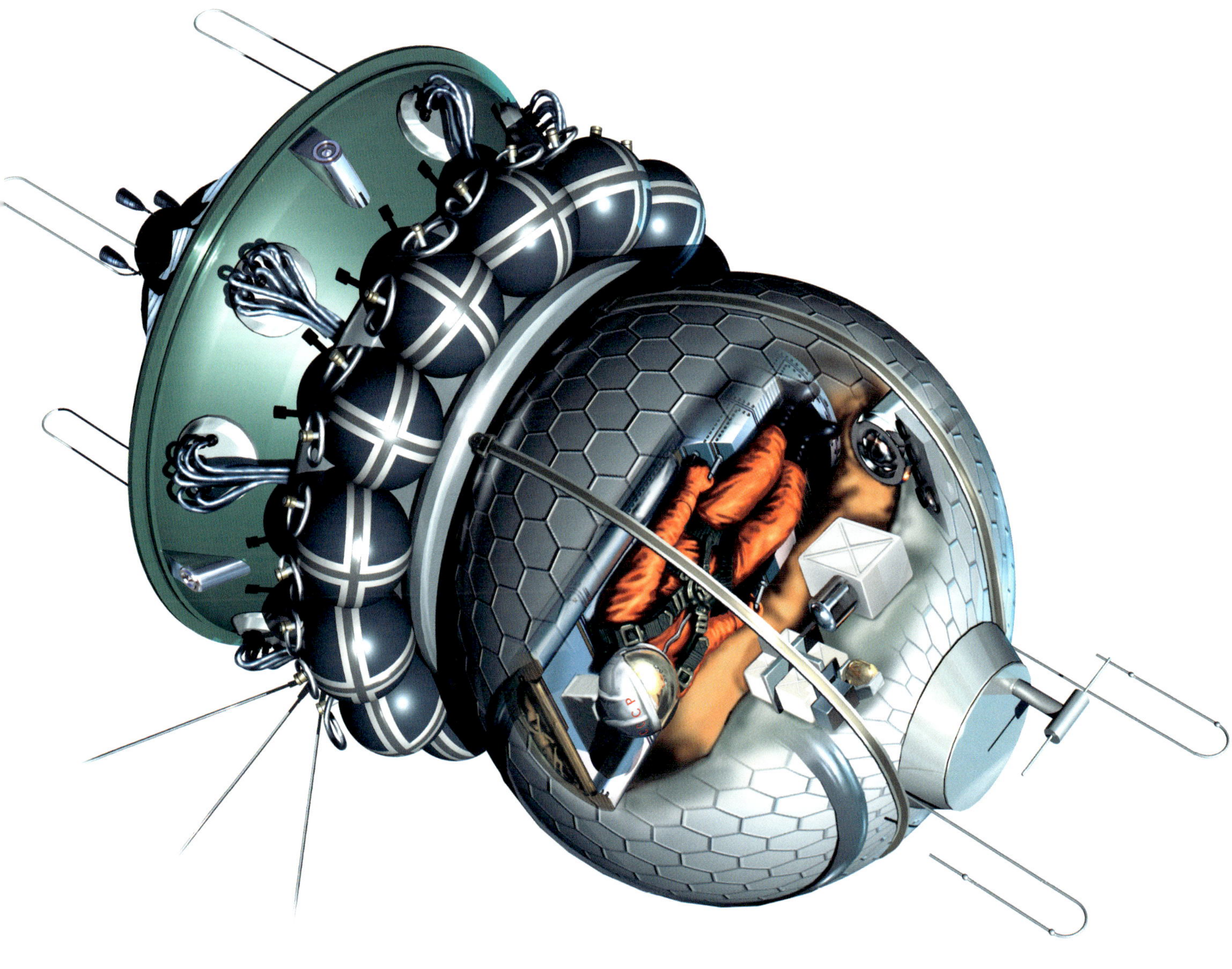

Cavendish Square

Published in 2025 by Cavendish Square Publishing, LLC
2544 Clinton Street, Buffalo, NY 14224

Website: cavendishsq.com

Series editor: Elizabeth Miles
Cover design: Duck Egg Blue
Illustrations and photographs: Jeff Bowles, David Hardy, Sebastian Quigley, Mike Saunders, Steve Weston, Gerald Witcomb, NASA, NASA Images, NASA/CXC/M.Weiss, NASA/ESA/Northrop Grumman, NASA/GSFC, NASA/Johns Hopkins University Applied Physics Laboratory/Southwest Research Institute/Alex Parker, NASA Johnson, NASA/JPL, NASA/JPL-Caltech, NASA/JPL-Caltech/GSFC/JAXA, NASA/JPL-Caltech/SSC, NASA/JPL/Malin Space Science Systems, NASA/JPL/University of Arizona, NASA/JPL/University of Arizona/University of Idaho, NASA/JPL/DLR, NASA/Johns Hopkins University Applied Physics Laboratory/Carnegie Institution of Washington, NASA/Space Telescope Science Institute, Shutterstock.com (Dotted Yeti, Alex Mit, NASA Images, Vadim Sadovski, Nerthuz, Rashevska Nataliia, sumikophoto, Magdanatka)

Cataloging-in-Publication Data

Names: Clark, Stuart.
Title: Space / Stuart Clark.
Description: Buffalo, NY : Cavendish Square Publishing, 2025. |
Series: How it works | Includes index.
Identifiers: ISBN 9781502672032 (pbk.) | ISBN 9781502672049 (library bound) |
ISBN 9781502672056 (ebook)
Subjects: LCSH: Outer space--Juvenile literature. | Astronomy--Juvenile literature.
Classification: LCC QB46.C537 2025 | DDC 523--dc23

CPSIA compliance information: Batch #CSCSQ25: For further information contact Cavendish Square Publishing LLC at 1-877-980-4450.

Printed in the United States of America

Contents

Big Bang 6
The Universe 8
The Solar System 10
The Planets 12
Planet Earth 14
Rocket Power 16
Early Missions 18
Project Apollo 20
On the Moon 22
Space Shuttle 24
Spacewalking 26
Space Stations 28
Viking Lander 30
Mars Pathfinder 32
Voyager 34
Studying the Stars 36
Stars 38
Black Holes 40
Radio Telescopes 42
Magnetic Fields 44
Index 46

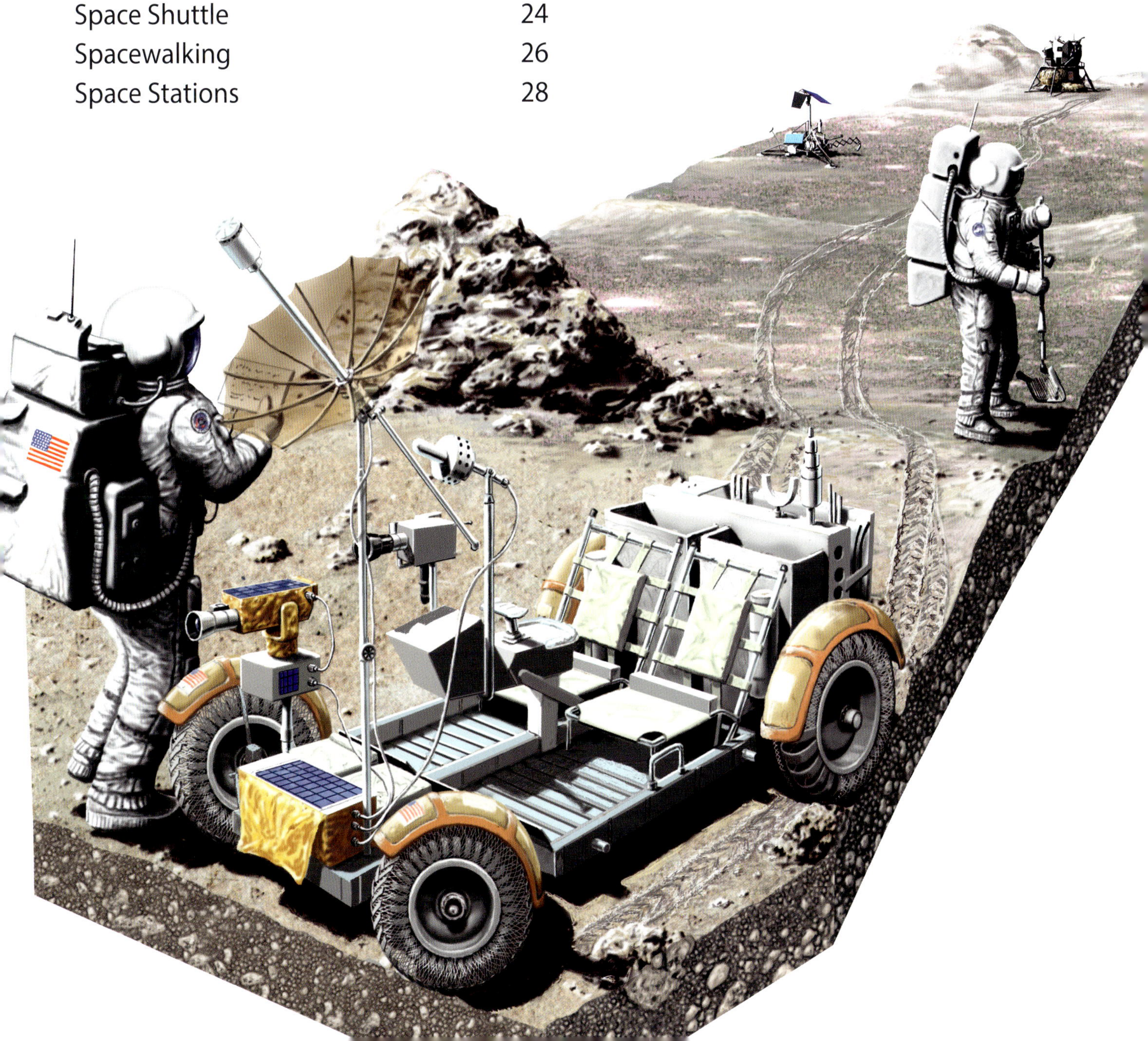

Big Bang

Astronomers believe that the universe began about 13.7 billion years ago with an event known as the Big Bang. At the time of the Big Bang, the universe began as the smallest of points and then suddenly began to expand. In about the same amount of time as it would take you to read this page, all the matter (material) that became everything we see today in the universe was created. Even the particles that make up this book were formed in the first few seconds after the Big Bang.

At first, everything was crammed into a tiny space, so the universe was very dense. At this point, atoms, the building blocks of matter, began to form. As time went by and the universe expanded more, it became less dense. Today, space is mostly empty, with dense parts (the planets, stars, and galaxies) only dotted around here and there.

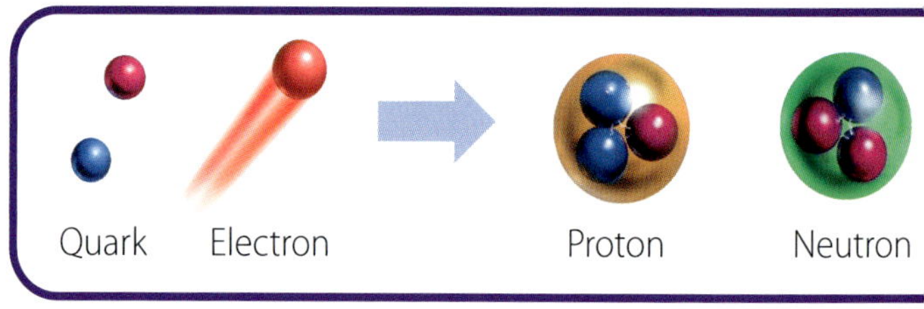

Formation of matter

A millionth of a second after the Big Bang, simple particles called quarks and electrons appeared. Quarks then joined together to form neutrons and protons. A single proton is known as a hydrogen nucleus. Later, neutrons and protons joined together to make helium nuclei. Finally, electrons began to orbit these nuclei and turn them into atoms.

The first seconds

In the beginning, the universe was a frenzy of activity. Matter existed only in the form of electrons and simple particles called quarks. These quarks were not yet stable and kept turning into energy. The energy then turned back into quarks.

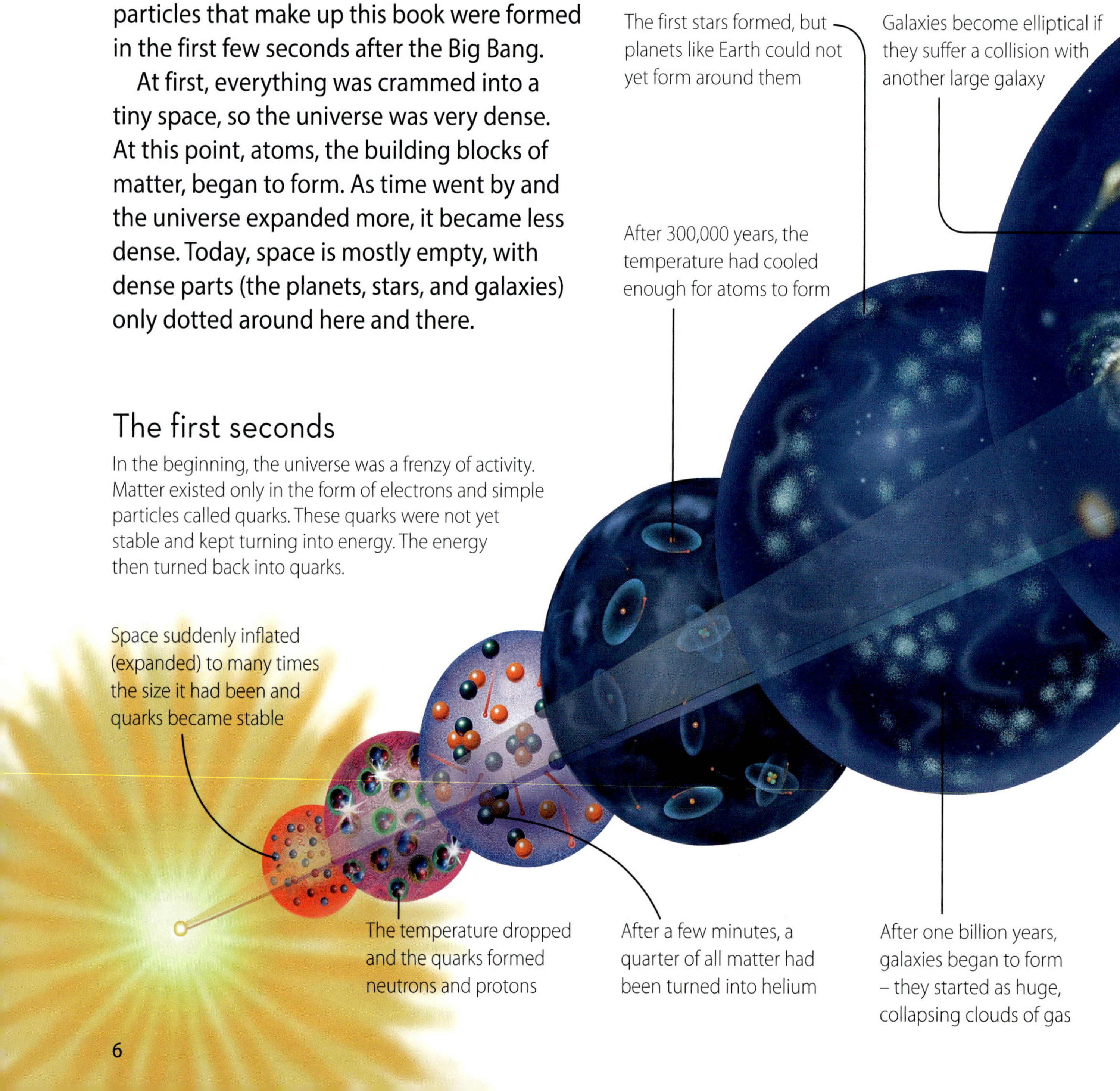

Birth of a planetary system

Planetary systems such as ours formed when gas clouds in galaxies collapsed. First, a gas cloud began to shrink and a star began to form at its center (**1**). As the cloud collapsed further, gases gathered in a disk around the star (**2**). The gases in this disk collided and stuck together, gradually turning into dust grains. The dust grains continued to become larger in this way until, after tens of thousands of years, planets were formed and a planetary system was born (**3**).

The Universe

The universe is so large that astronomers measure most distances in light-years. One light-year is 5.9 trillion miles (9.5 trillion km) – the distance that light travels in a year. A ray of light travels at 186,000 miles (300,000 km) a second, which is faster than anything else in the universe.

There are many different types of objects found in the universe. Some are very large and others are tiny. The largest are gigantic filaments, which are made up of superclusters. These contain clusters (groups) of galaxies. Galaxies are the homes of stars. A spiral galaxy, such as our Milky Way galaxy, is about 100,000 light-years across. Some galaxies are still forming new stars today, but others stopped making stars millions of years ago. Planets can be found orbiting (moving in a circular path around) some stars. The smallest solid objects in the universe are the tiny particles of dust that lie between the planets.

Types of galaxies

Galaxies can be split into three types: elliptical galaxies (**1**); spiral galaxies, like Andromeda, with curved arms of stars (**2**); and barred-spiral galaxies which have a bar of stars between their arms and their centers (**3**).

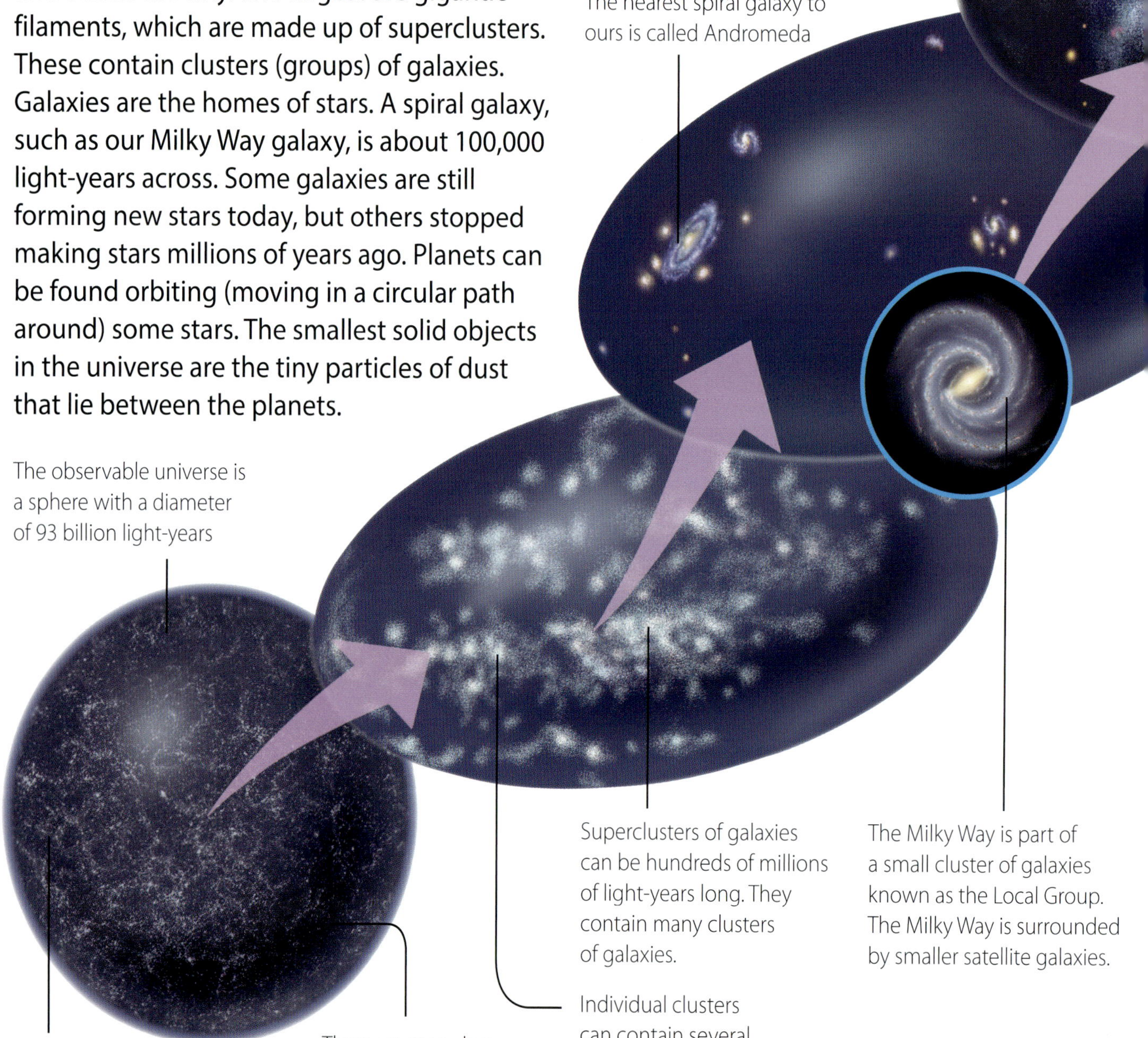

The expanding universe

In the 1920s, astronomers Edwin Hubble and Milton Humason showed that the universe was expanding. They were studying galaxies and noticed that the light from them was being stretched. This stretching affects the colors of light from galaxies in an effect called redshift. The further away the galaxy, the greater its redshift. This stretching of light is caused by the expansion of space. The further away the galaxy is, the more space there is between us and it that can expand. Astronomers now use redshift to measure the distances between galaxies.

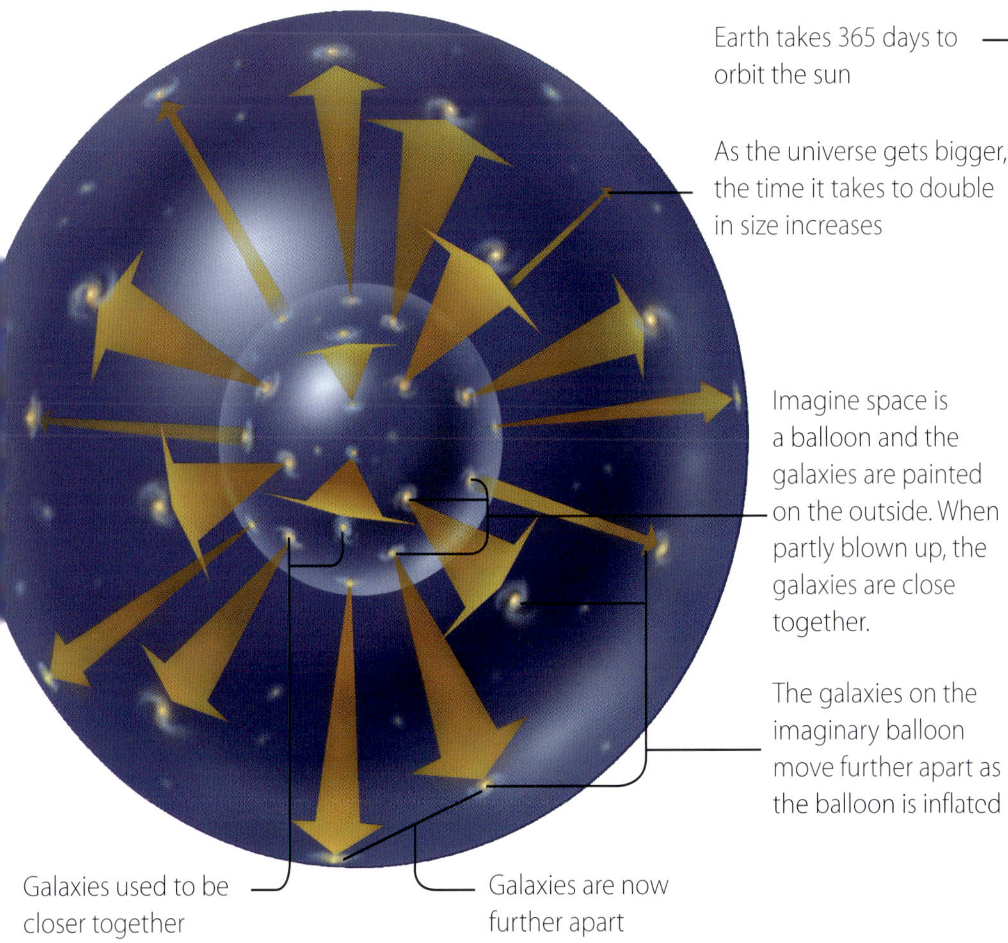

The Solar System

We live on Earth. Earth belongs to a family of eight planets that orbit the sun. Both the planets and the sun formed about 4.6 billion years ago and together they are known as the solar system. The four inner planets – Mercury, Venus, Earth, and Mars – are all similar. They are rocky worlds, but only Earth has an atmosphere (the gas surrounding a planet) that humans can breathe.

Beyond Mars is the asteroid belt. This band contains millions and millions of rocks that also orbit the sun. Still further away are four larger planets: Jupiter, Saturn, Uranus, and Neptune. These "gas giants" have very thick atmospheres and no solid surfaces. Jupiter is the largest planet. Beyond the gas giants is Pluto, which was once called a planet but is now classed as a "dwarf planet," along with other small, icy worlds that orbit in the outer part of the solar system.

The Galaxy

The sun is one of billions of stars which make up our galaxy. Also known as the Milky Way, the galaxy has a flat, spiral shape. The sun is not at its center. In fact, it is in one of the spiral arms, closer to the galaxy's edge than its center. Its location is shown by the red dots below. The sun orbits the center of the galaxy once every 220,000,000 years. Our galaxy is one of billions in the universe.

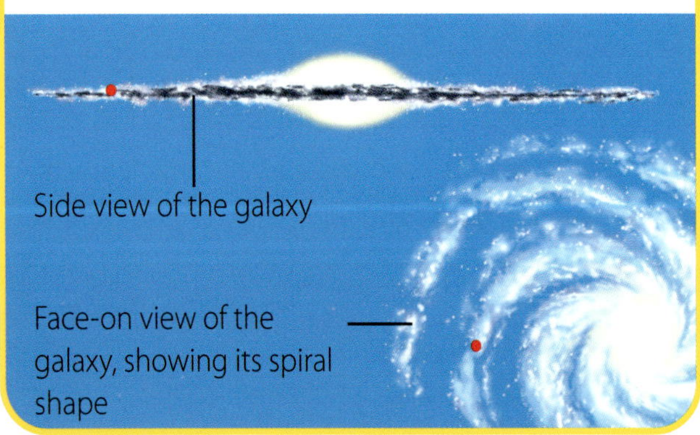

Orbits

The planets are held in the solar system by the pull of the sun's gravity. The sun contains so much matter that its force of gravity is very large and causes the planets to move in orbits around it. The patterns of these orbits are similar to circles.

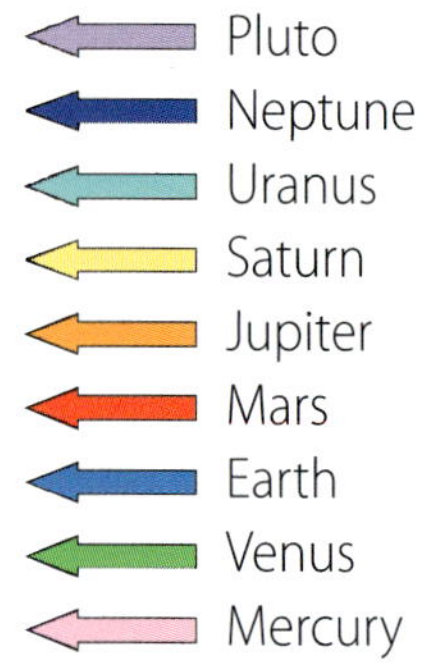

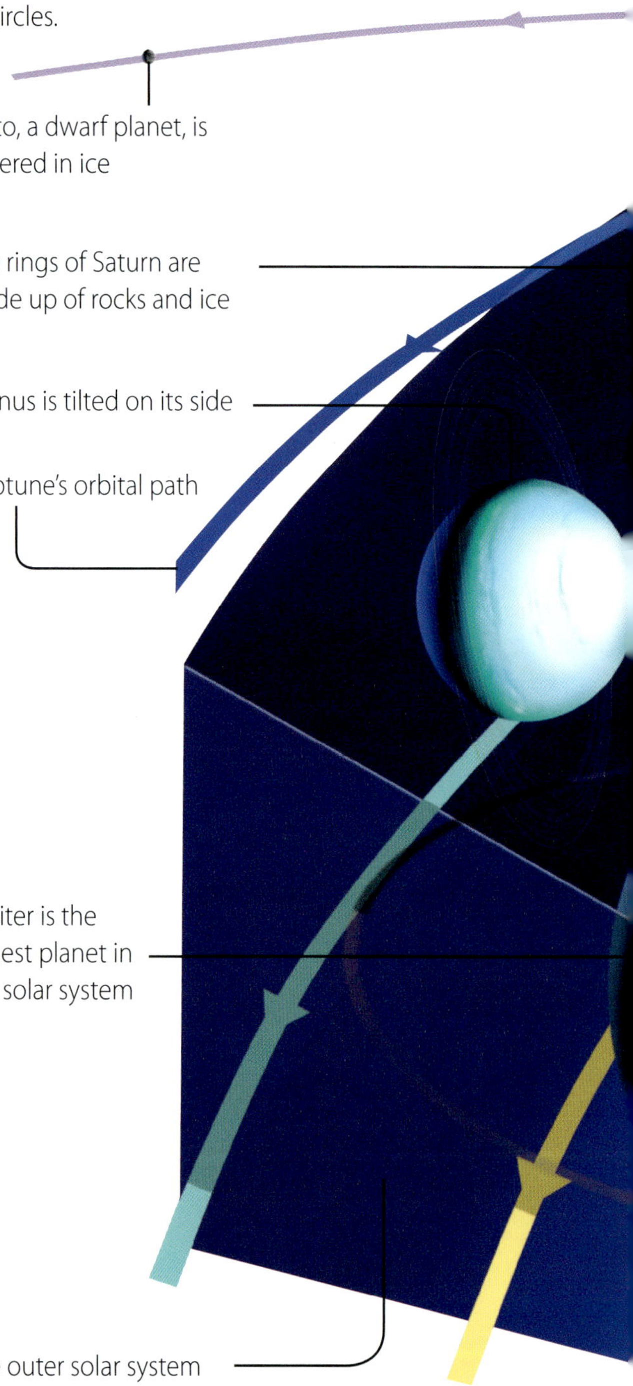

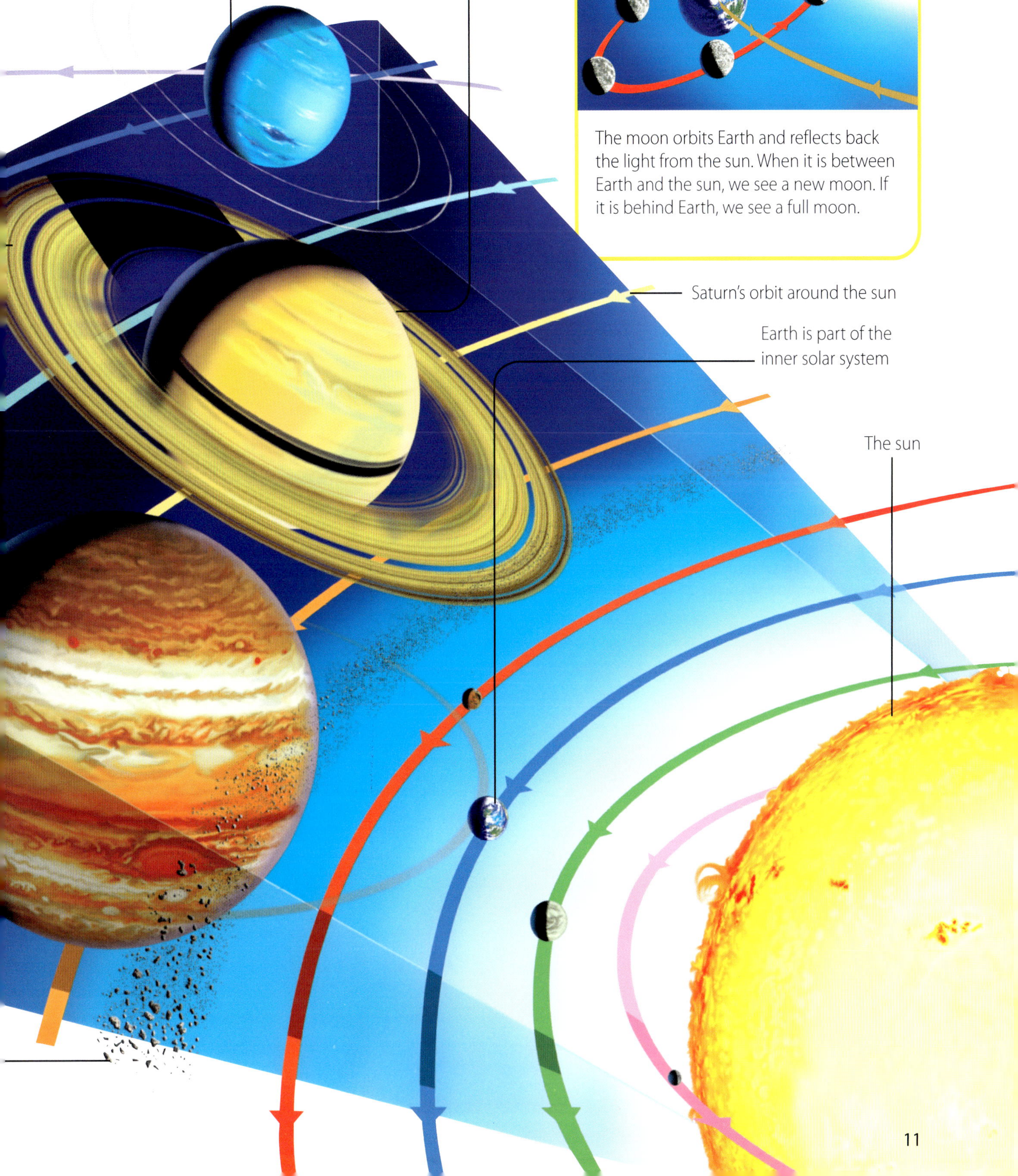

The moon's phases

The moon orbits Earth and reflects back the light from the sun. When it is between Earth and the sun, we see a new moon. If it is behind Earth, we see a full moon.

The Planets

All eight planets of the solar system orbit the sun but each one is unique. Many have moons in orbit around them. The four gas giants – Uranus, Jupiter, Neptune, and Saturn – have rings as well.

The matter inside a planet or moon is found in layers. The densest material is at the center and is usually made up of iron. The outer material consists of rocks. Gas, which is a planet's lightest material, sits above the planet's surface and is known as the atmosphere. This layering of the planets and moons shows that when they formed, they were made of molten lava (collisions with other new planets had made their rocks melt). While they were molten, the heavy material would easily sink to the center and the light material would float to the surface.

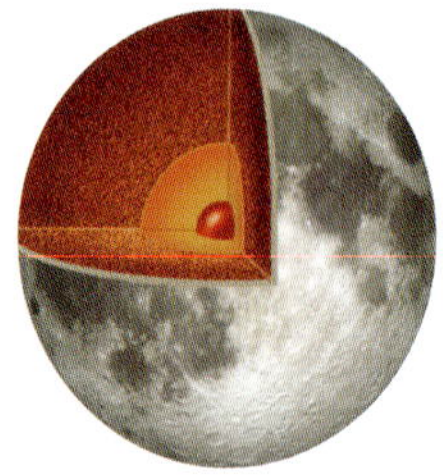
(1)

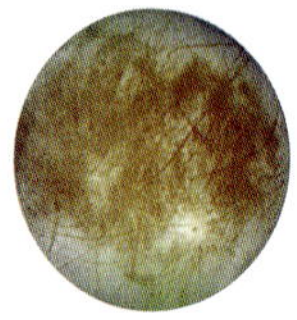
(2)

(3)

(4)

Moons

Earth's moon is rocky with a small iron core (1). There are many other natural satellites, mostly around the gas giants. Jupiter's moons include Europa (2), which scientists think has an ocean beneath its icy crust, and Io (3), which has the most volcanoes in the solar system. Saturn's largest moon, Titan (4), is always covered in clouds.

Jupiter's Great Red Spot is a storm as large as Earth

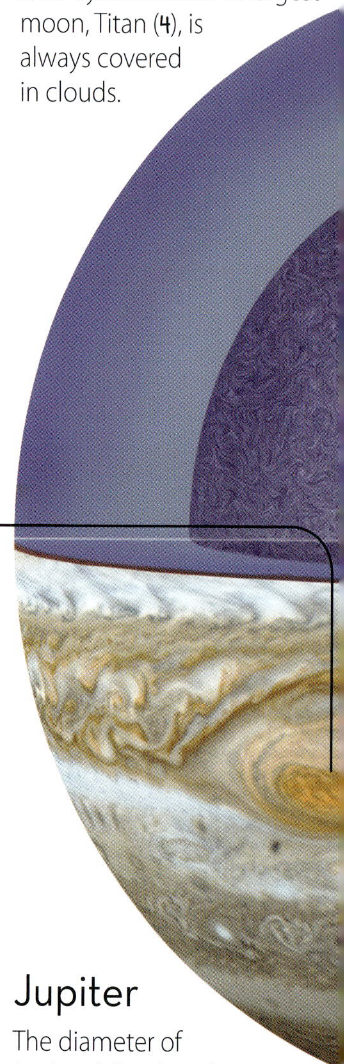

Pluto's moon, Charon, was discovered in 1978

Pluto

Pluto (*above*) is a dwarf planet. It is much smaller than Earth, and is made up of ice surrounding a core of rock and iron. It is orbited by five natural satellites, the largest of which is Charon.

Uranus

This blue-green gas giant (*below, right*) has a thick atmosphere of gas over an even thicker icy layer of water, methane, and ammonia, with a small rocky core about the size of Earth at its center.

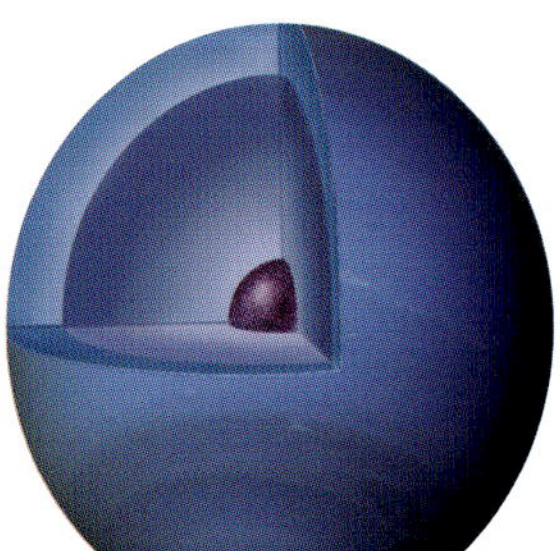

Neptune

The planet Neptune (*left*) is about the same size as Uranus. It also has a similar inner structure. The rings of Neptune are patchy. Some areas are rather dense while others are sparse.

Narrow rings around Uranus are made up of small, dark dust particles

Jupiter

The diameter of Jupiter (*above*) is eleven times that of Earth. Below the surface of Jupiter, a mixture of hydrogen and helium gas is squeezed so much it behaves like a liquid. Below this, the mixture is squeezed even more and acts like a liquid metal. In the very center of the planet there may be a rock and iron core five times bigger than Earth.

Mercury

Mercury (*left*) is the closest planet to the sun. It has a large iron core, covered by a layer of rocky material. On top is the crust, cratered by collisions with smaller objects such as asteroids.

Venus

Venus (*left*) is almost the same size as Earth but is very different in other ways. It is permanently covered in clouds of carbon dioxide and its surface is hotter than an oven.

The clouds around Venus hide a landscape of cliffs, valleys, highlands, and lowlands

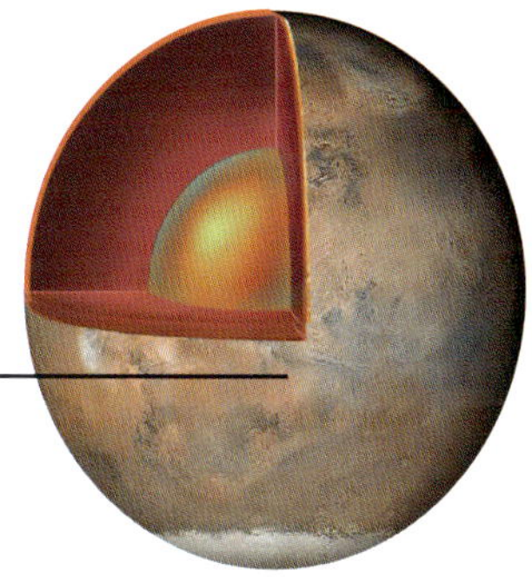

The Mariner Valley is about 13,100 miles (4,000 km) long

Mars

The diameter of Mars (*above*) is about half that of Earth. It has a very large rift valley called the Mariner Valley, named after the space probe that discovered it.

Saturn is the flattest of the planets. Its squashed sphere shape is caused by its low density and fast rotation

Saturn's rings have gaps caused by the gravity of its moons

Saturn

The interior of Saturn is similar to that of Jupiter. One difference between them is that inside Saturn it is possible for helium gas to become a liquid. It then falls as rain into the central region of the planet.

Planet Earth

Earth is the planet on which we live. It formed with the sun and other planets 4.6 billion years ago. Originally, Earth was a sphere of lava (molten rock). Heavy chemicals such as iron sank into the planet, while lighter ones floated to the top. Water and the atmospheric gases that allow us to live and breathe were brought to the planet by colliding balls of ice known as comets.

Earth has a core of iron surrounded by a large region of molten rocks, called the mantle. Heat traveling through the outer mantle causes the molten rocks to move in large, oval pathways. The rocky crust of Earth is broken into large pieces called plates. These float on the mantle. Where they collide, earthquakes occur and volcanoes erupt.

Earth's core

Earth's core contains one-third of our planet's mass. Geologists have monitored the way in which sounds travel through Earth and discovered that the core is divided into two regions. The outer core is made up of liquid iron. The inner core is solid iron.

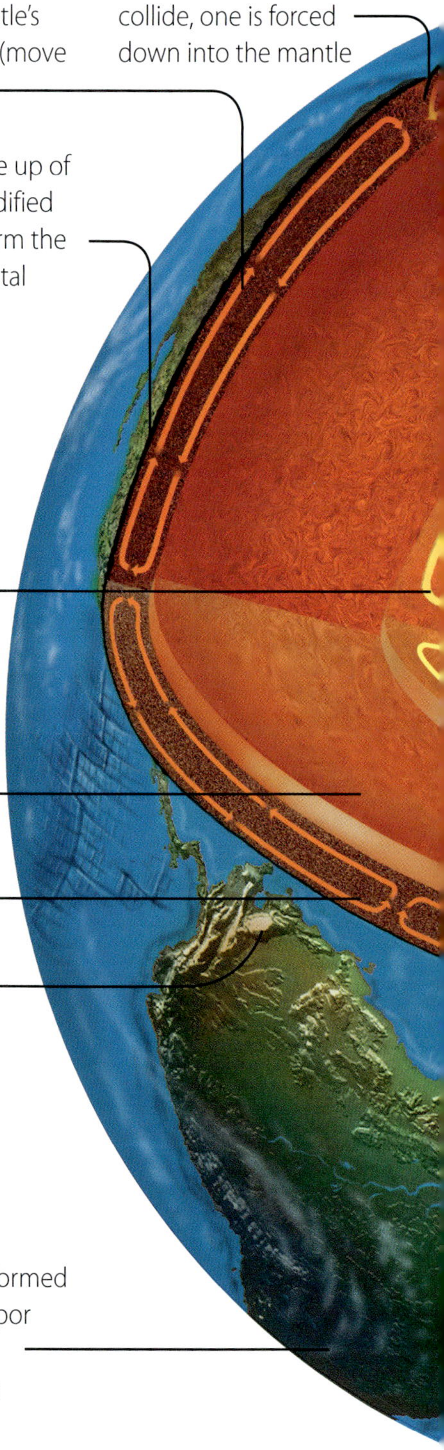

The seasons

As it orbits the sun, the spinning Earth is always tilted at the same angle. When the North Pole is tilted towards the sun, it is summer in the north (1). Six months later, it is tilted away and it is winter (2). In between are the seasons spring (3) and autumn (4).

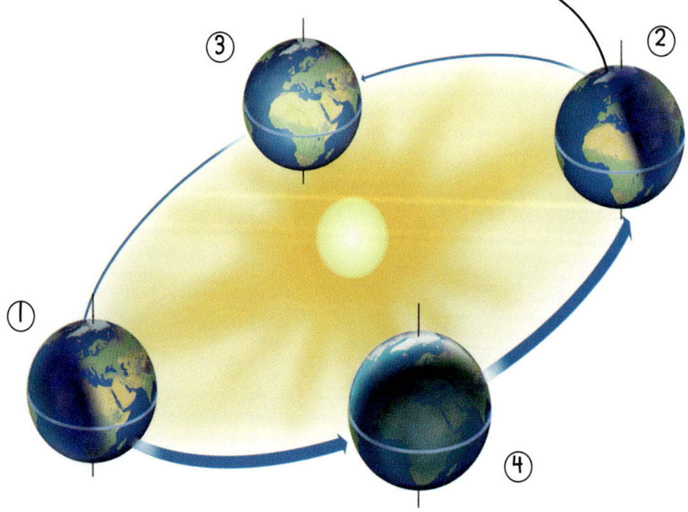

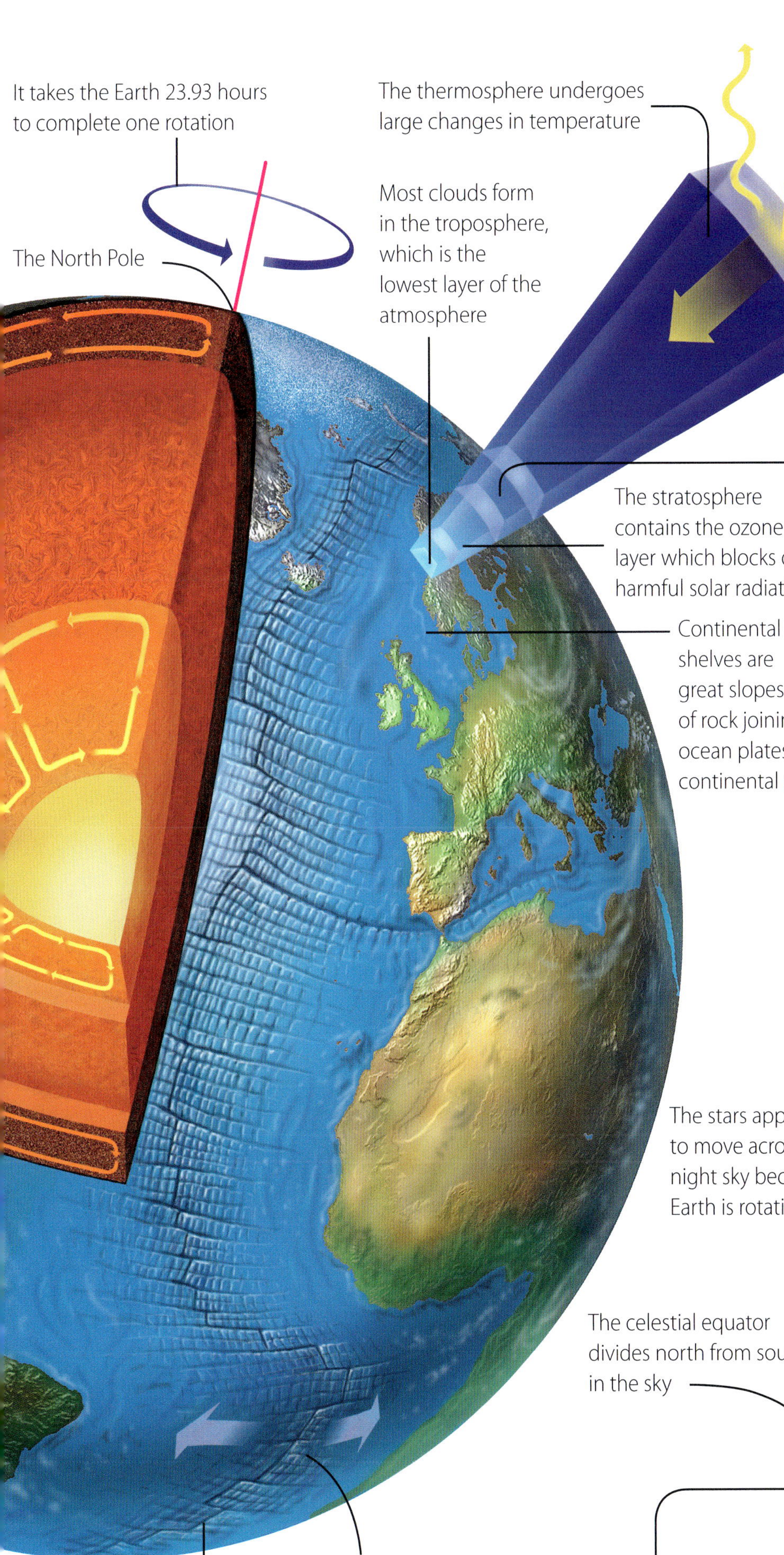

The atmosphere

Earth's atmosphere is the blanket of gases surrounding the planet. It insulates the planet, keeping it warm. It also blocks out most of the sun's harmful radiation such as ultraviolet light. Most importantly, it allows us to breathe.

The celestial sphere

From Earth it looks as if the stars are painted onto a huge sphere surrounding the planet. This is called the celestial sphere. Throughout the year the nighttime side of Earth faces various directions in space, so different stars on the sphere are seen.

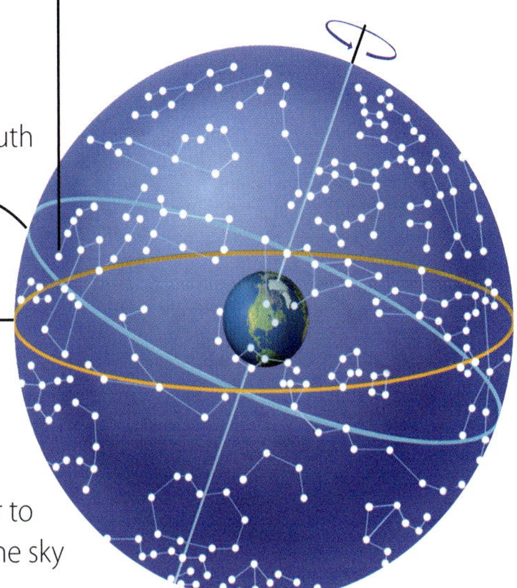

Rocket Power

The concept of the rocket can be traced back to ancient Greece in the 4th century BCE. In the 13th century AD, the Chinese built rockets made of gunpowder and bamboo tubes. They attached these to arrows and launched them. In peaceful times, rockets were used as fireworks, but during wars they were weapons.

The principle behind how a rocket works is that every action creates an equal and opposite reaction. This was stated as a law of motion by Sir Isaac Newton in 1687. If an explosion produces gas and that gas can be directed out of a tube, the gas leaving the tube will cause the tube itself to move in the opposite direction.

Rockets blast off from launch pads and take objects, such as communications satellites or a crew, into space. Some modern rockets, such as the Falcon 9 and Falcon Heavy, can return to Earth and land so they can be reused.

One of the most powerful rockets yet flown was the Saturn V, which launched astronauts to the moon; it was over 360 feet (110 m) high. NASA's Space Launch System (SLS) rocket is even more powerful.

Satellites that are taken into orbit are known as the payload

This satellite is a telescope to be placed in a low Earth orbit

Payloads must be designed to fit into the rocket from which they will be launched

Satellites may have small rockets of their own to place them in their final orbits

Ariane 4 was a European-built rocket, launched from South America. It was 200 feet (60 m) high.

Stages

Although early rockets consisted of single engines, scientists soon realized that rockets should be built in stages. A stage is a section of the rocket that falls away when its fuel is used up. This reduces the rocket's mass so that it can be accelerated more easily by the next stage's engines.

The Saturn V and Soyuz are three-stage rockets. The large first stage lifts the rocket from the ground. When its fuel tanks are empty, it is cast off and the second stage's engines take over. Finally, a third stage places the rocket and its payload into orbit.

History of rockets

Early in the 20th century, American Robert Goddard launched the first modern rocket (1). It flew to a height of 41 feet (12.5 m). Rockets have always been used as weapons and in World War II the Germans developed the V-2 rocket (2) to launch attacks on London. Many countries have developed rockets. Russia built the R-7 family of rockets to launch their Vostok and Soyuz missions (3). The Saturn V rocket (4) was developed by America for the Apollo Moon missions, and the Space Shuttle (5) was the first reusable spacecraft.

Flight path

The Ariane rocket took off (1) using the first stage and the strap-on boosters. When the boosters were out of fuel they were cast off (2). Shortly afterwards, the first stage also ran out of fuel and was dropped (3). The fairing split (4) in preparation for releasing the satellites. The second stage used its fuel and was discarded (5). The first satellite was deployed (6) into a low Earth orbit (7). The second satellite was boosted to a much higher orbit (8).

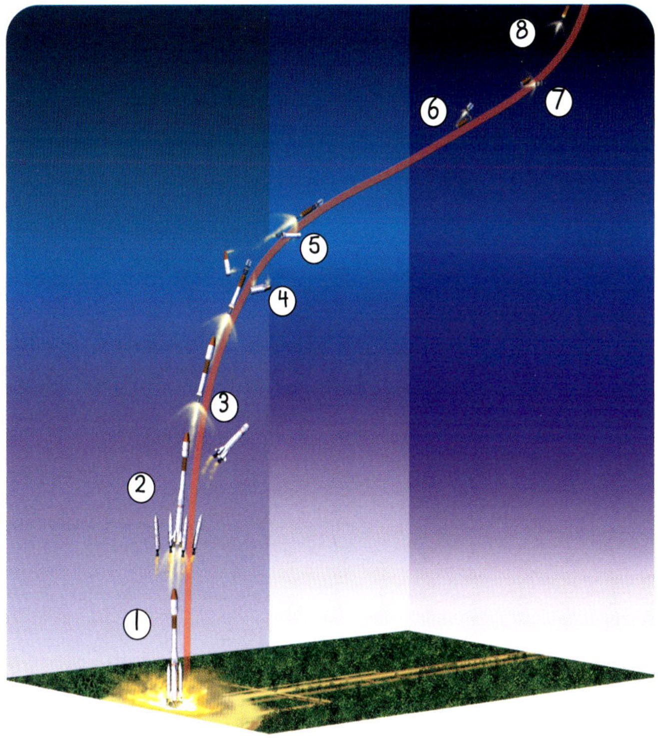

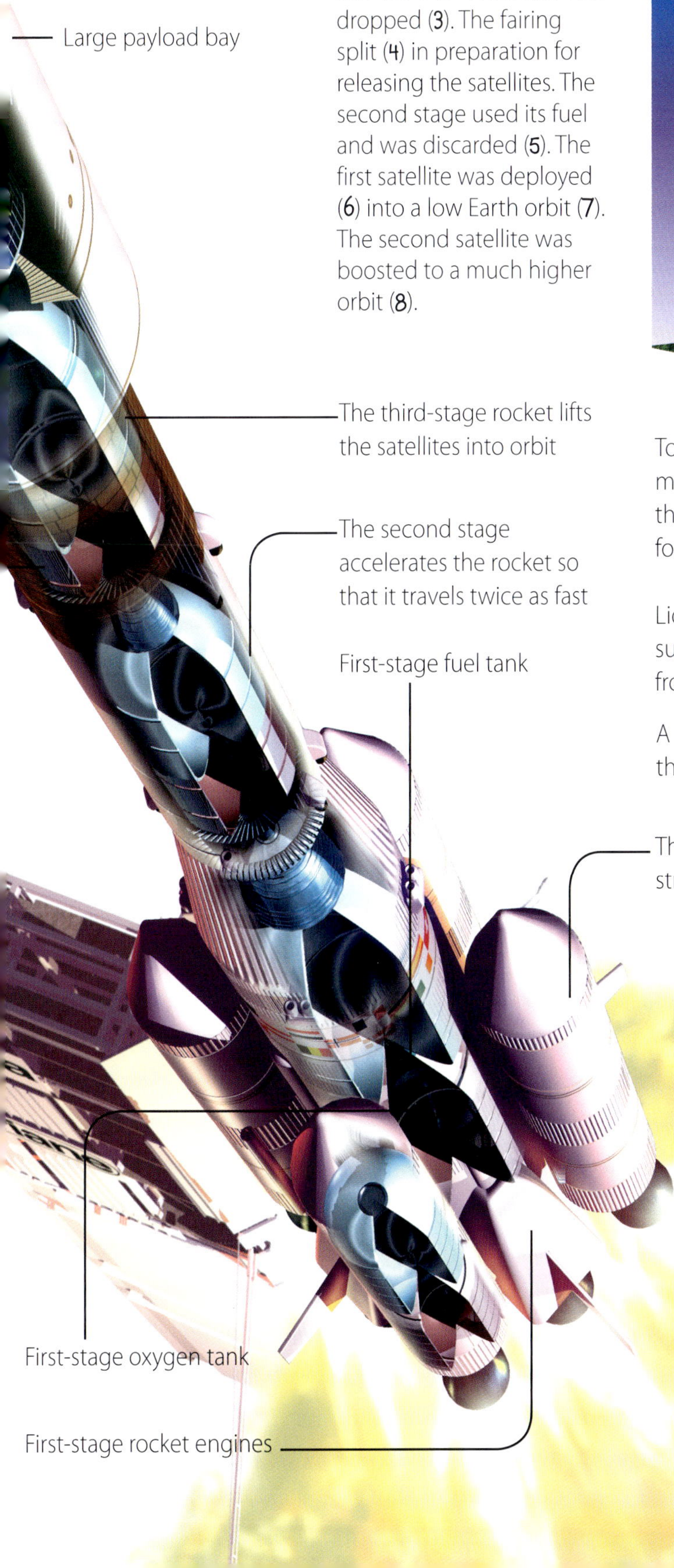

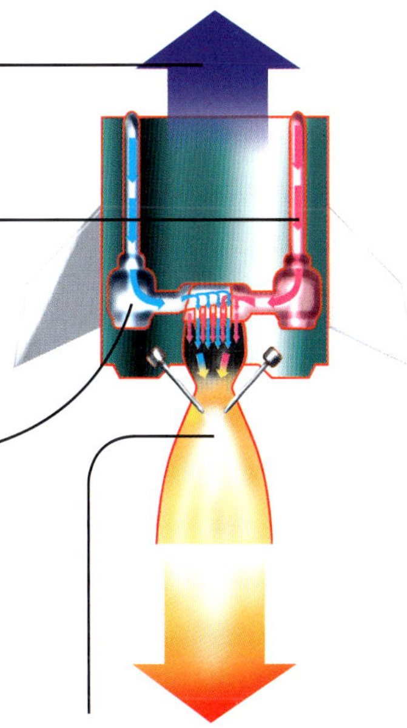

Rocket fuel

Rocket engines ignite fuel to produce thrust. Liquid oxygen mixed with another liquid fuel, such as hydrogen or fluorine, produces more thrust than a single fuel could. In the future, rockets may use three fuels and gain even more energy.

Early Missions

The Soviet Union (now Russia) was the first country to place a human being in space. The cosmonaut Yuri Gagarin flew in the spacecraft Vostok 1 on April 12, 1961. His flight lasted just 89 minutes, but during that time he made a complete orbit of Earth and then returned safely. Vostok 1 had been launched from what is now Kazakhstan by a rocket designed as a missile to carry explosives. The Russians launched Vostok 2 just a few months later on August 6, 1961. This time the cosmonaut stayed in space for a whole day.

A year later the Russians launched cosmonauts in Vostok 3 and 4 with just 24 hours between the launches. Both spacecraft successfully returned to Earth a few days later. In 1963, Vostok 5 and 6 were launched. Vostok 6 carried Valentina Tereshkova, the first woman in space.

Flight profile

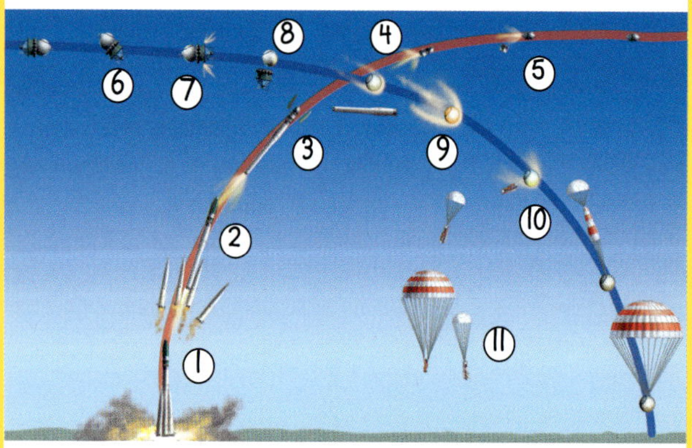

Vostok 1 blasts off (1) and drops the first-stage boosters (2). The nose casing is ejected as the second stage accelerates Vostok's speed (3). The final stage puts it in orbit (4) and then separates (5). After an orbit Vostok turns (6) and fires its retro-rocket (7). The instrument module is discarded (8) and Vostok 1 reenters the atmosphere (9). The cosmonaut is ejected (10). Parachutes return the module and astronaut safely to Earth (11).

The instrument module

The instrument module was controlled by the scientists on the ground. It was equipped with rocket engines that could control the spacecraft movement once it was in orbit. Communication antennae were also attached to it. The module was ejected and allowed to burn up during reentry to Earth.

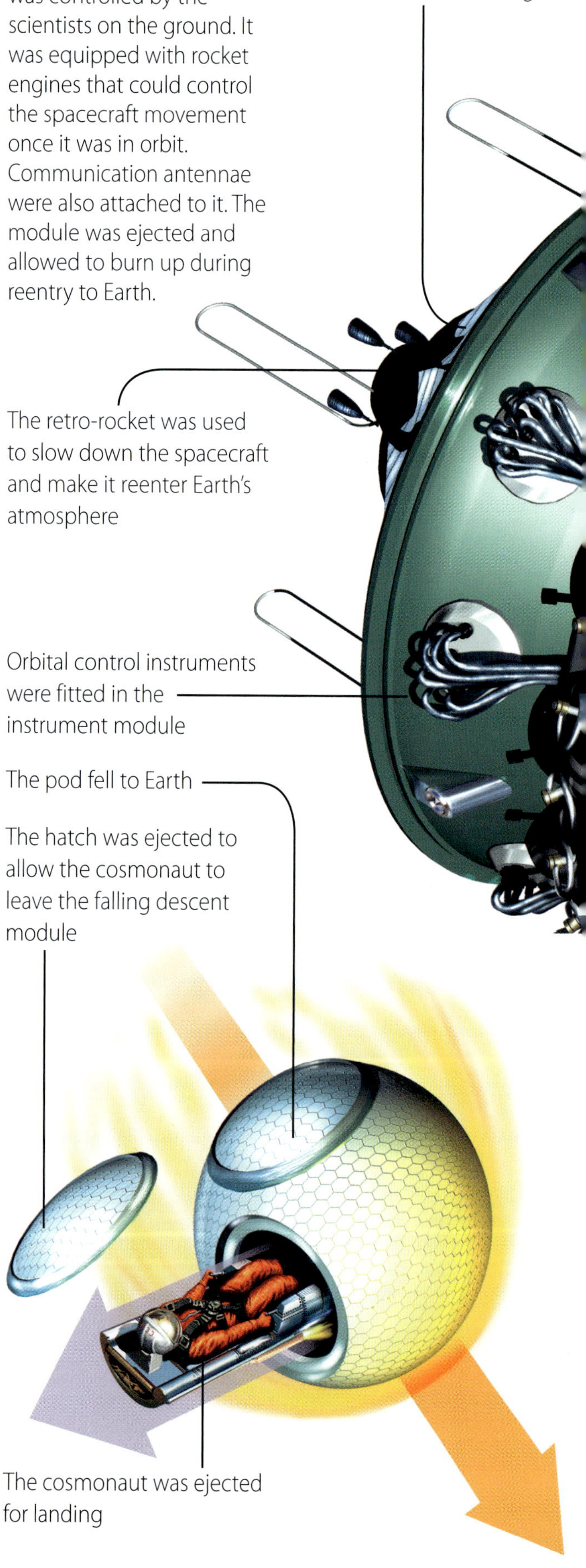

Delivery to orbit

Exactly 156 seconds after liftoff, the nose casing surrounding the Vostok module fell away. Then, 300 seconds after liftoff, the second stage fell away and the final stage of the launch rocket ignited. Its rocket engine burned for the next 376 seconds and put the craft into orbit. There the spherical capsule and the conical instrument module were released.

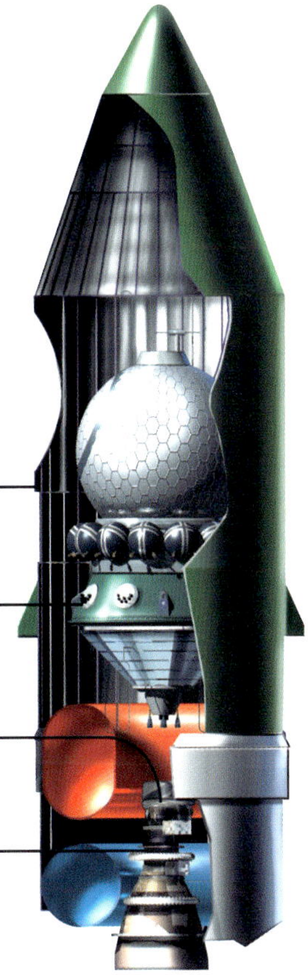

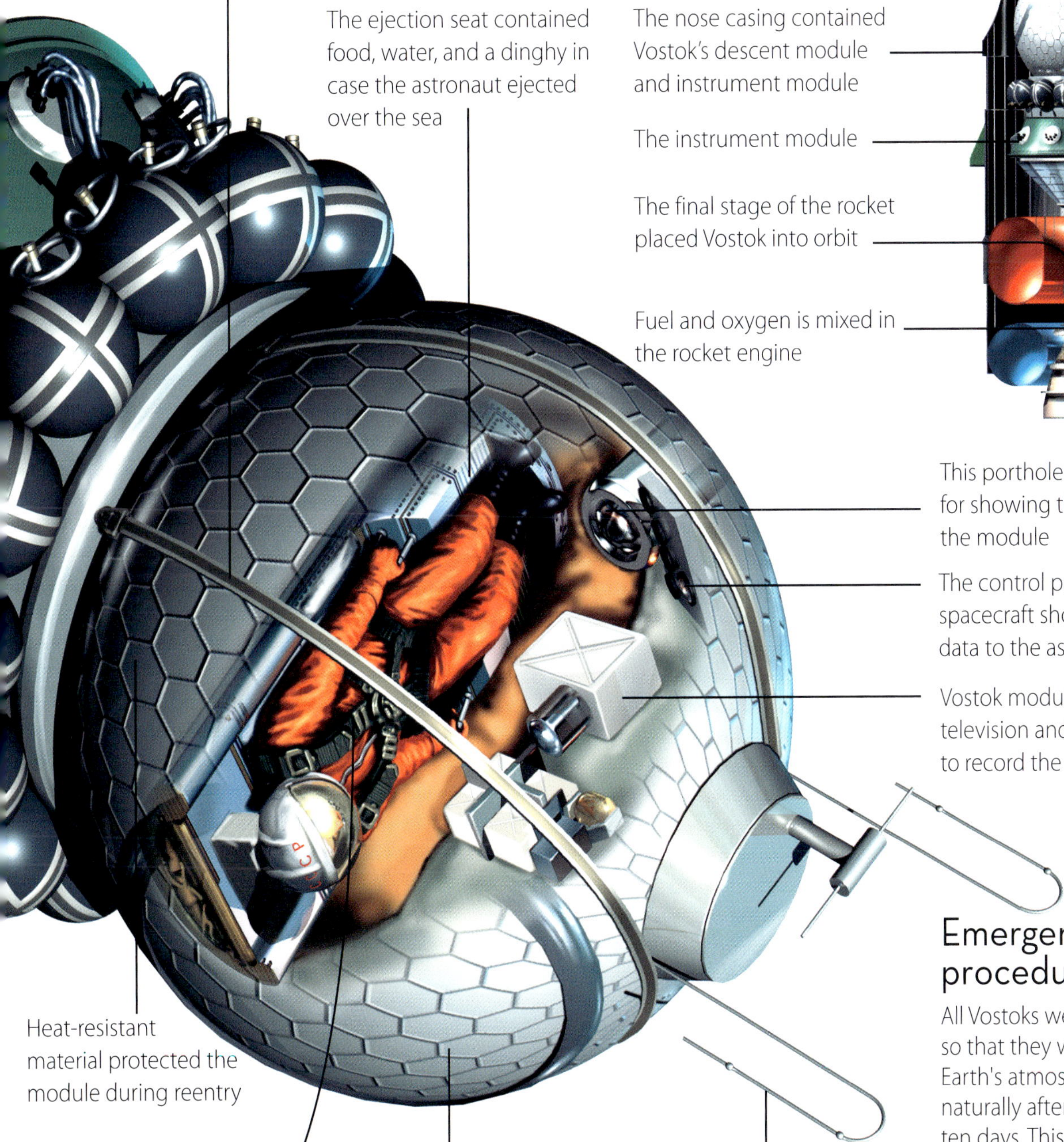

Emergency procedure

All Vostoks were launched so that they would reenter Earth's atmosphere naturally after a period of ten days. This prevented the loss of the cosmonaut's life should the retro-rocket fail to slow the spacecraft down. In order to survive for ten days, the Vostok capsule was stocked with enough food and water, but this precaution was never needed.

Astronaut ejection

The Vostok modules landed on solid ground. Although the module was slowed by parachutes, the impact might have hurt the cosmonaut inside. So the cosmonaut was ejected and came down by parachute separately.

Project Apollo

One of the greatest achievements of the human race has been the space missions of the late 1960s and early 1970s, which placed humans on the moon. On July 20, 1969, Apollo 11 touched down on the moon. Shortly afterwards, astronaut Neil Armstrong became the first human being to walk on a world in the solar system other than Earth.

Over three years, seven manned missions were launched to land on the moon. Each carried three astronauts. One stayed in the command module and orbited around the moon while the other two descended to the surface in the lunar module.

Apollo 13 almost became a disaster when an electrical system short-circuited and caused an explosion, destroying an oxygen tank. The landing on the moon was abandoned and the astronauts were returned safely to Earth. They used oxygen from the lunar module to keep themselves alive.

Arriving at the Moon

When the Apollo spacecraft arrived at the moon it was made up of the command and service module (CSM) and lunar module joined together. With the CSM facing backwards, its engine was fired to put the spacecraft into lunar orbit. Two astronauts climbed into the lunar module. The lunar module then separated and fired its engine. This began the descent to the surface of the moon to land.

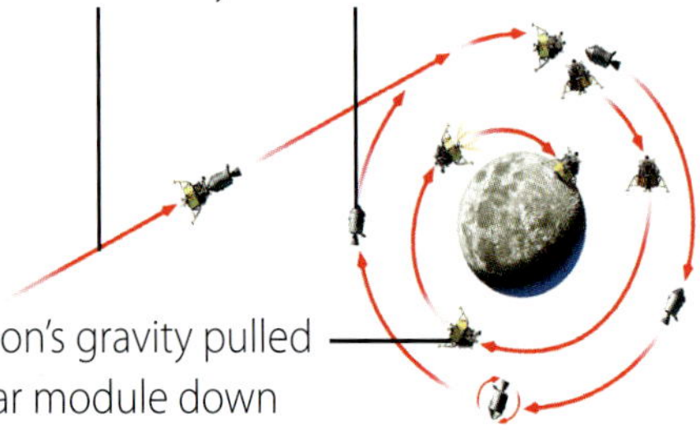

Command and service module

The command and service module was the astronauts' home during the voyages to and from the moon. The conical section at the front is the command module, where the astronauts sat. It separated from the service module and reentered Earth's atmosphere when the mission was complete.

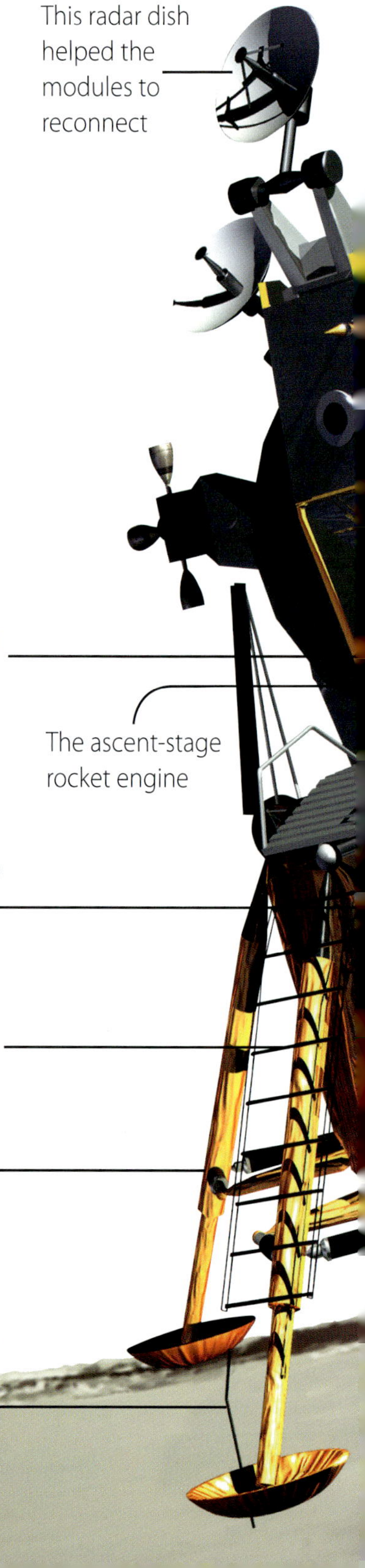

Back to Earth

When the moon walks were completed, the ascent stage of the lunar module lifted off and docked with the command and service module. The ascent stage was then undocked and allowed to fall back onto the moon. The astronauts then traveled back to Earth.

Firing its main engine put the command and service module on a course back to Earth

The lunar module

The lunar module (*left*) was the small spacecraft that carried the astronauts down to the surface of the moon. It was made up of two parts, or stages. On top was the ascent stage. This contained the astronauts' cabin and the controls to fly the lunar module. Underneath was the descent stage, which had space to store equipment to be used on the moon.

When it was time to leave the moon, the descent stage was left behind. Because the force of gravity is less powerful on the moon than it is on Earth, the ascent stage only needed a smaller engine to take off.

On the Moon

After Apollo 11 touched down on the moon's surface, the astronauts prepared to go outside. During this first crewed moon landing, the astronauts made one trip outside the lunar module. Their moon walk lasted two and a half hours. Then they climbed back aboard and prepared for takeoff.

On each of the Apollo missions that followed, the astronauts spent longer and longer on the moon. For Apollo 15, 16, and 17, each crew made several journeys away from the lander and spent over 18 hours exploring. Apollo 17, in December 1972, was the last manned mission to the moon. Since then, ice has been discovered on the lunar surface. In the future, this could be used to provide drinking water and to produce rocket fuel to make longer stays possible.

Moon walking

While they were on the surface of the moon, the astronauts performed many tasks. They collected rock samples and also left packages of experiments behind that continued to send information back to Earth long after the astronauts had left.

Portable life support system

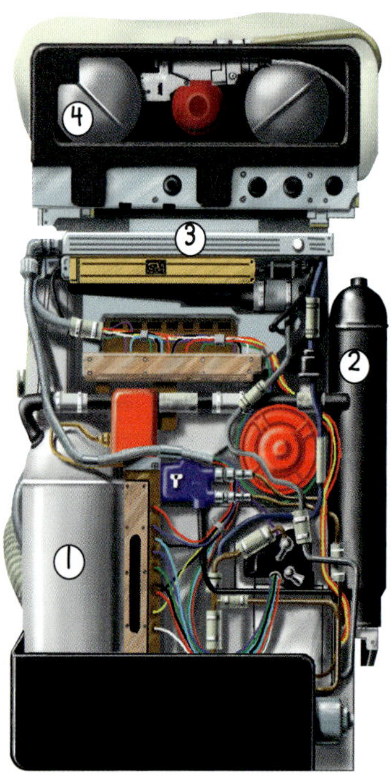

Because the moon is so small, its gravity would not be strong enough to hold air around it. This means that astronauts have to wear spacesuits to stay alive. The Apollo spacesuit was connected to a backpack called the Portable Life Support System (PLSS). The PLSS pumped oxygen (1) and water (2) to the spacesuit so that the astronaut could breathe and keep their body temperature normal. A radio (3) enabled the astronauts to talk to each other. An emergency oxygen supply (4) was also included.

Surveyor probes

Before humans set foot on the moon, Surveyor landers were sent there. Cameras on the spacecraft took pictures of the surface – these helped scientists to choose Apollo landing sites.

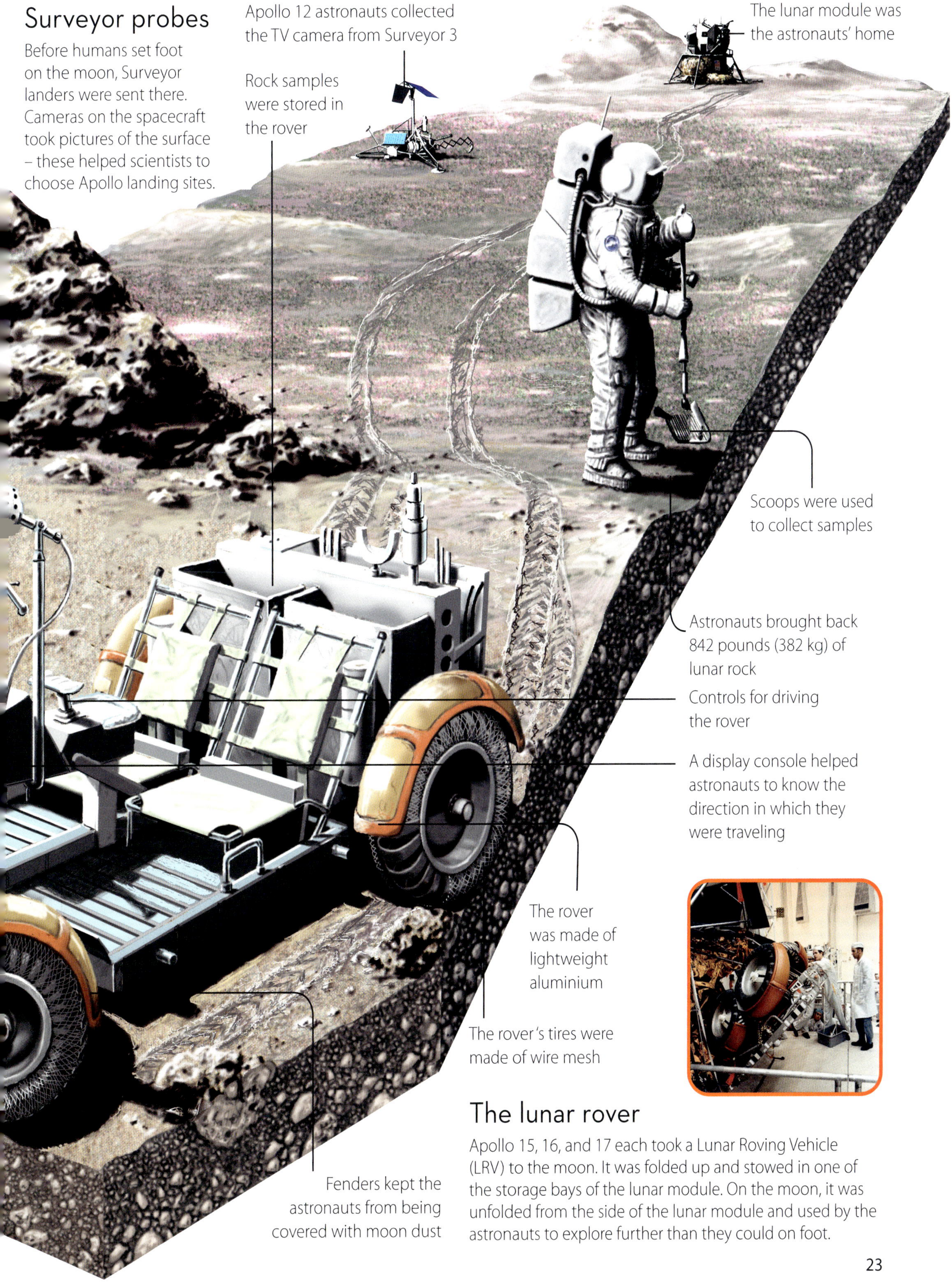

The lunar rover

Apollo 15, 16, and 17 each took a Lunar Roving Vehicle (LRV) to the moon. It was folded up and stowed in one of the storage bays of the lunar module. On the moon, it was unfolded from the side of the lunar module and used by the astronauts to explore further than they could on foot.

Space Shuttle

The Space Shuttle was the first spacecraft that could be used more than once. In the early days of space exploration, spacecraft were only able to fly a single mission. Most parts of the rocket burned up in the atmosphere or were left in space. The first Space Shuttle, called *Enterprise*, never flew in space but proved that such a large craft could glide successfully down to Earth.

The second Space Shuttle, *Columbia*, was launched in 1981. This was followed by *Challenger*, *Discovery*, *Atlantis*, and *Endeavour*. In 1986, *Challenger* exploded shortly after takeoff, tragically killing all seven astronauts on board. In 2003, *Columbia* disintegrated during reentry into Earth's atmosphere at the end of its 28th mission. Again, the crew were lost.

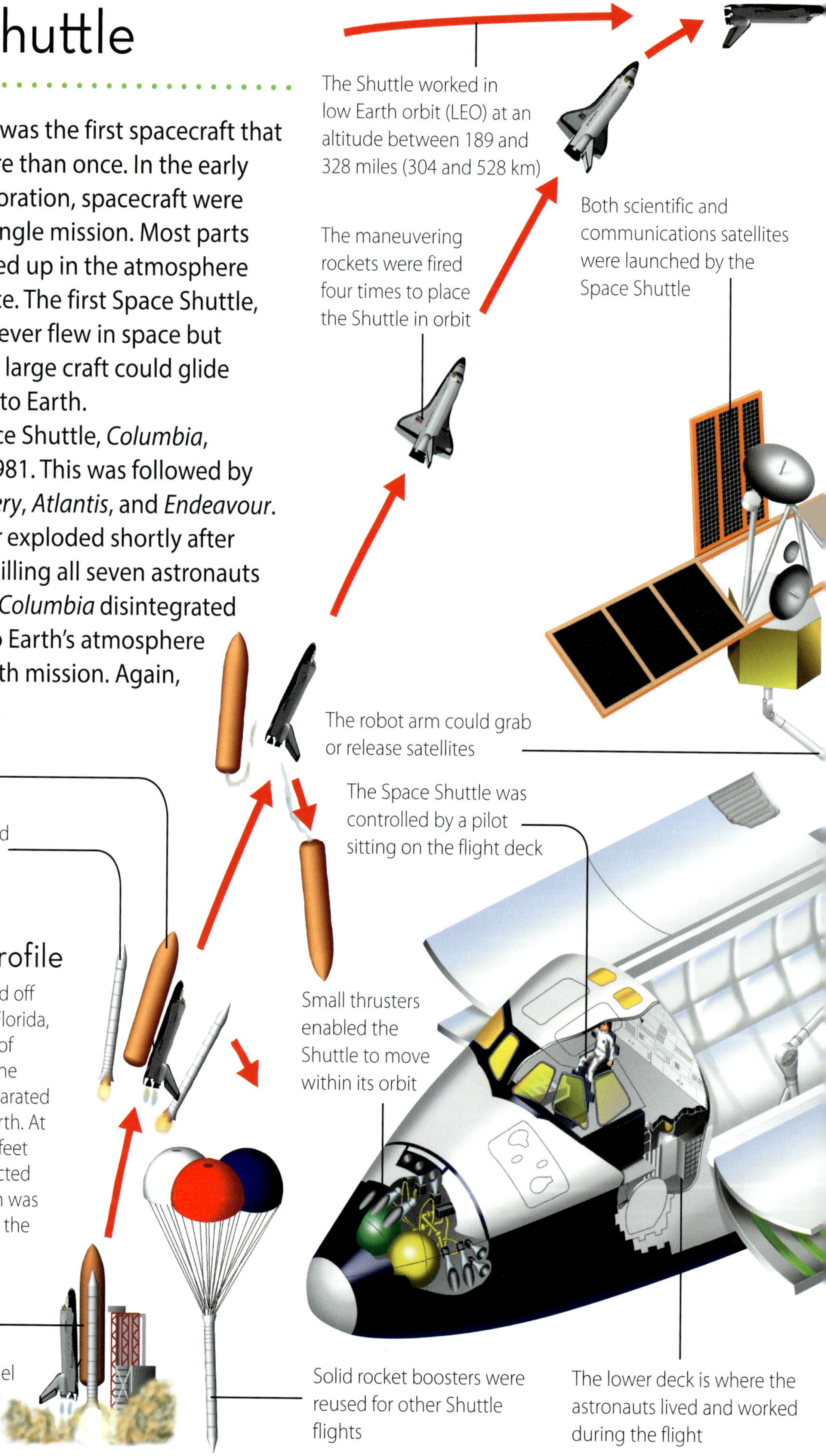

Shuttle flight profile

The Space Shuttle blasted off from Cape Canaveral in Florida, in the U.S. At an altitude of about 164 feet (50 km), the solid rocket boosters separated and fell back down to Earth. At an altitude of about 394 feet (120 km), the Shuttle ejected the main fuel tank, which was now empty. At this point the Shuttle was moving fast enough to reach orbit.

Satellites

Many satellites work in much higher Earth orbits than the Space Shuttle could take them. Some were even sent to other planets. So satellites had to fire their own smaller rockets after the Shuttle had put them into space.

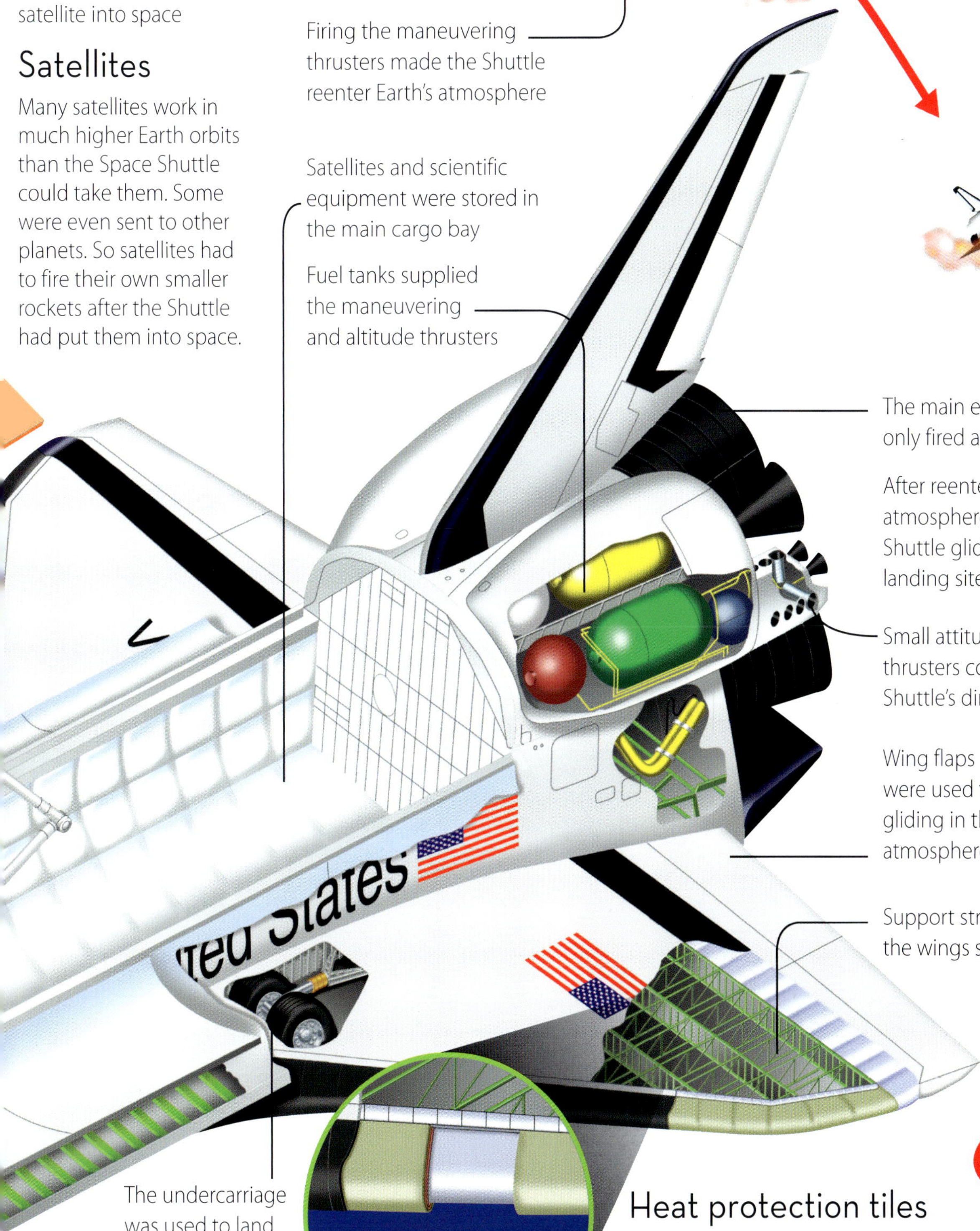

Heat protection tiles

As the Shuttle reentered the atmosphere, friction raised its surface temperature enormously. The Shuttle was covered in protective tiles to prevent damage. The tiles could withstand temperatures of 2,012°F (1,100°C).

Shuttle landings

Previous crewed American spacecraft splashed down in the ocean. The Space Shuttle landed like an airplane, making it possible to reuse.

Spacewalking

There is no atmosphere for humans to breathe in space. Whenever work needs to be done outside a spacecraft, astronauts have to put on a spacesuit. Spacesuits keep the astronaut's body at the right temperature and supply them with oxygen to breathe and water to drink. On Earth, the pressure of the atmosphere prevents the fluids in our bodies from turning into gases. In space, a spacesuit must be pressurized to keep the astronaut's body fluids liquid.

On Earth and inside spacecraft, only one-fifth of the gas breathed is oxygen, but in a spacesuit all of the gas is oxygen. Before astronauts can go outside, they must spend over two hours breathing nothing but oxygen through a mask in order to get used to it.

Moving in space

On three Shuttle missions, to move around in space, astronauts had to wear a backpack, called the Manned Maneuvering Unit (MMU). It was fitted with small thrusters that were controlled by handheld levers. The left control lever was used to make the spacewalker go forwards or backwards. The right hand lever controlled the direction the astronaut faced. It could make them turn left or right, up or down, or twist around clockwise or counterclockwise.

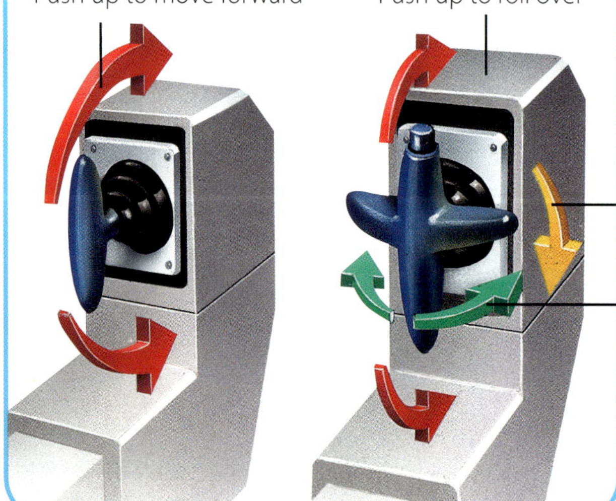

Attitude jets

The attitude jets pushed the spacewalker along by blowing out nitrogen gas. The astronaut decided which way to move and pulled or twisted the control levers. A computer calculated which jet should be fired. For example, to make an astronaut turn, more than one jet was fired at the same time.

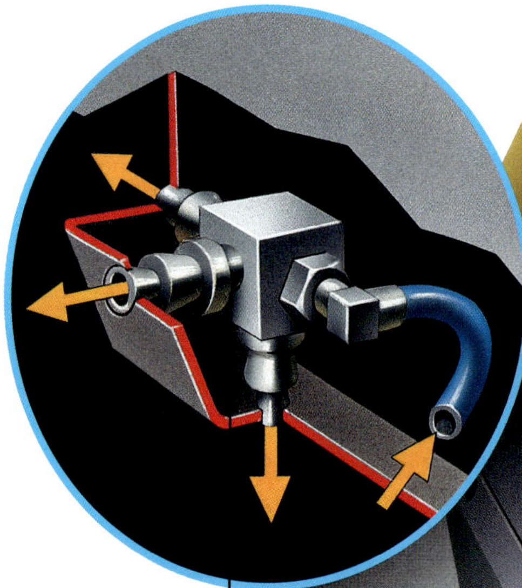

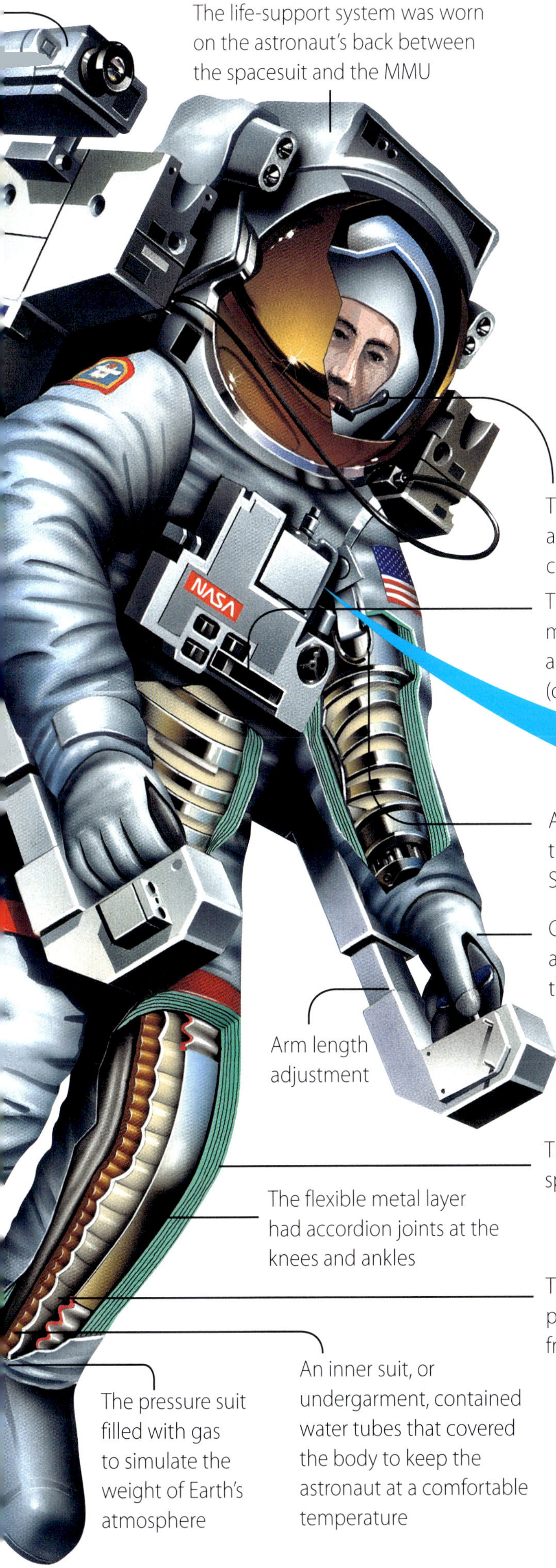

Spacesuit control box

The controls to manage every aspect of the spacesuit were located on a box mounted on its front. If astronauts wanted to talk over the radio, they selected a channel (**1**), adjusted the volume (**2**), and pressed the switch to talk (**3**). If they were too hot or cold, they could adjust the temperature of their spacesuit (**4**). More or less oxygen could be supplied by using a sliding control (**5**) and their water supply could be adjusted (**6**).

Space Stations

In 1971, the Soviet Union launched the first space station, Salyut 1. Early space stations only stayed in orbit for a few months, but as better systems were developed, they stayed in orbit for longer. The Russian space station, Mir, remained in orbit from 1986 to 2001.

The U.S. launched the Skylab space station in 1973. Three crews of astronauts worked there for a total of 172 days. Almost six years later, in 1979, Skylab eventually burned up in Earth's atmosphere. The International Space Station (*below* and *right*) is maintained by the U.S., Russia, Canada, Japan, and 11 countries of the European Space Agency. It continues to be modified as technology advances and mission requirements change.

Habitation module

The habitation module is one of the most important parts of the space station because it is where the astronauts live and sleep. Astronauts sleep near vents which take away the carbon dioxide they breathe out.

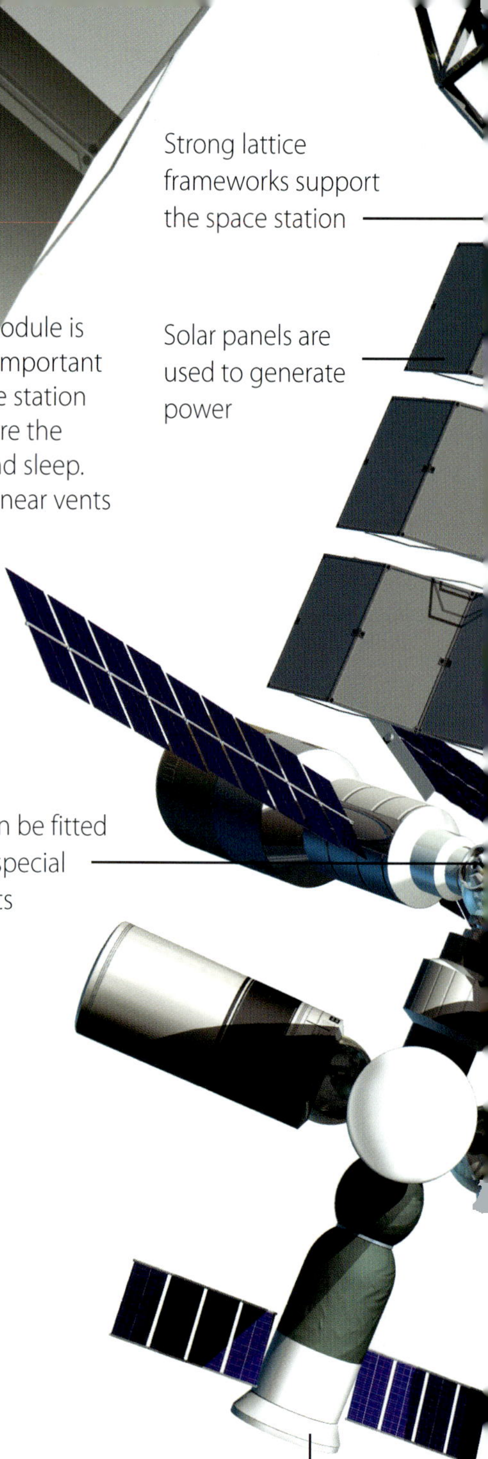

Space station construction

The International Space Station (*above* and *right*) has been constructed over several years. The first stage was the delivery of the central connecting structure (1) in 1998. During the second stage, three astronauts boarded the station (2). In the third stage, many of the scientific modules were added (3). In the year 2000, a full-time crew finally occupied the station for the first time (4).

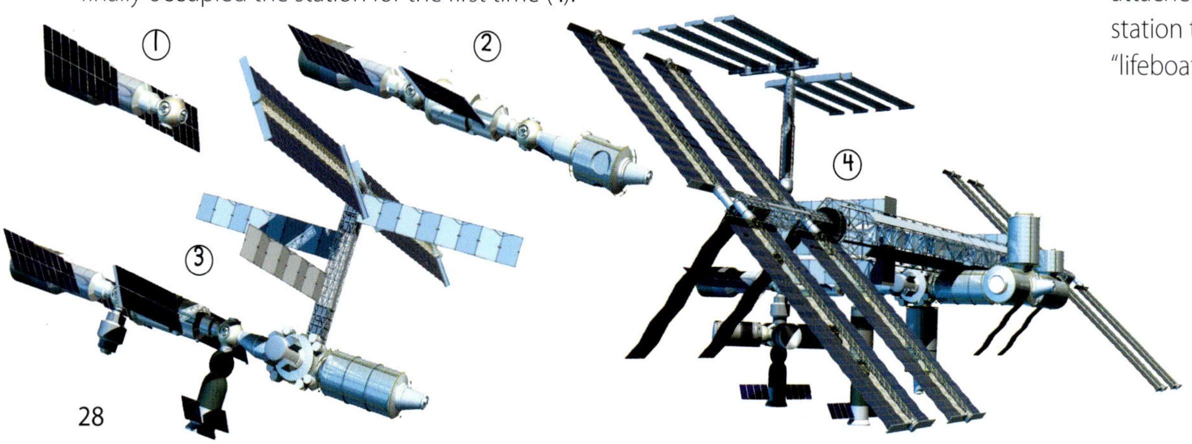

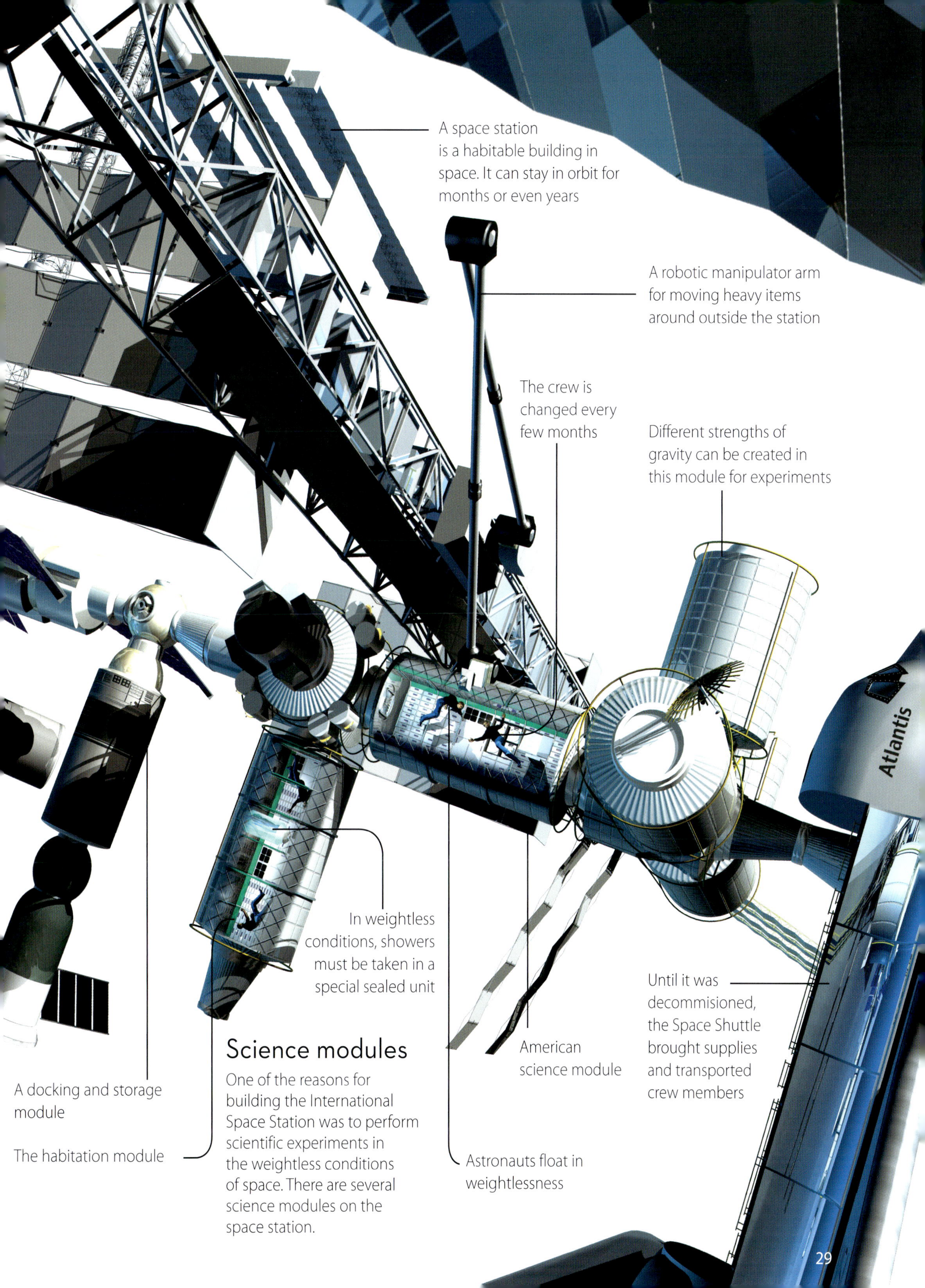

Science modules

One of the reasons for building the International Space Station was to perform scientific experiments in the weightless conditions of space. There are several science modules on the space station.

Viking Lander

The Viking missions were the first to have landers successfully touch down on the surface of Mars. The project was begun in 1968. Because there was a risk of the Viking spacecraft breaking down, two were built. If one didn't work, the other could carry on with the mission. In fact, both space probes worked very well. They landed in the summer of 1976 and worked for many years. Along with the landers, each of the Viking space probes had a section that stayed in orbit. Together, the two Viking orbiters surveyed and mapped nearly all of the planet's surface.

Many scientists think that Mars was once very like Earth. There is evidence that parts of its surface were once covered in water. This means that life may have started on Mars too. The Viking landers had special equipment on board to test the soil in case it contained tiny living organisms called microbes. But the tests did not find evidence of any form of life.

The Viking landings

The site of Viking I's touchdown was Chryse Planitia, near the Martian equator. Viking II landed further north in Utopia Planitia. Both areas are flat and desertlike. Heavily cratered areas were avoided in case they damaged the landing spacecraft.

This antenna sent information to Earth and received commands

The cameras observed a test pattern to get their color balance right

Magnets on the test chart were sensitive to magnetic activity on Mars

A machine for measuring earthquakes didn't detect any on Mars

Viking used two cameras to take pictures of the Martian surface

Power generators under protective cover

Fuel tank

Martian soil is red in color because it is covered in iron oxide, or rust

Flight path

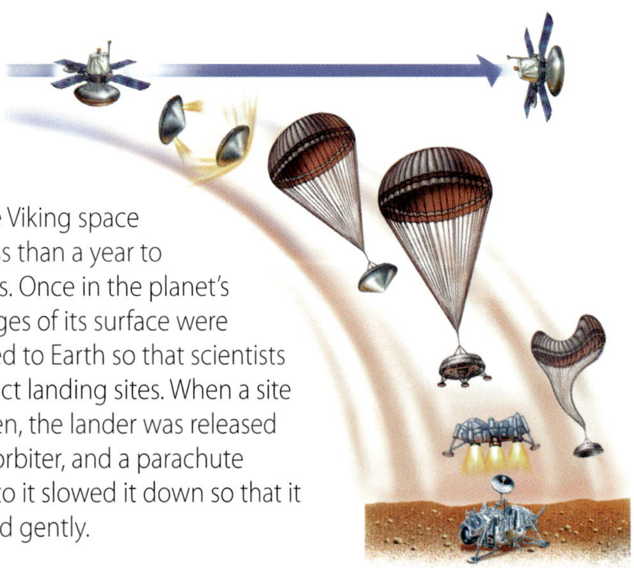

It took the Viking space probes less than a year to reach Mars. Once in the planet's orbit, images of its surface were transmitted to Earth so that scientists could select landing sites. When a site was chosen, the lander was released from the orbiter, and a parachute attached to it slowed it down so that it would land gently.

Pictures of Mars

Viking I began transmitting pictures (like the photo *above*) to Earth just 25 seconds after it touched down on Mars. Because of the long distance from Mars to Earth, the pictures took 19 minutes to arrive by a radio signal. One picture showed a large rock. NASA scientists called it "Big Joe." There were fewer big rocks in the region where Viking II touched down.

The robotic arm

Viking was designed to test the surface of Mars for signs of life. It did this by scooping soil from the surface and dropping it into the biology processor and heating device. The robotic arm was sent commands from Earth and then carried them out automatically.

Mars Pathfinder

The Mars Pathfinder mission landed on Mars on July 4, 1997. It was the first spacecraft to land on the planet since Viking 1 and 2. There are rock features on Mars that could only have been produced by flowing water. Yet, today, there seems to be hardly any water on the planet. It is hoped that missions like the Mars Pathfinder will help us to find out what happened to it. Pathfinder was a success and returned data for several weeks, even though conditions on Mars were harsh.

Mars Pathfinder was the first mission in an ambitious program of space probes that will visit Mars. Another, called the Mars Global Surveyor, was sent shortly afterwards to map the planet. Since then, larger rovers Spirit and Opportunity, and the car-sized Curiosity, have all explored even more of Mars's surface. In July 2020, NASA launched Mars 2020, sending another rover similar to Curiosity, called Perseverance, and a small helicopter, Ingenuity, to investigate the surface and look for evidence that there was once life on Mars.

Mars landscape

Mars Pathfinder was designed to land on an ancient floodplain. It is estimated that the flood took place several billion years ago. The surface has remained virtually unchanged since then. The lander came to rest in a small dip. Mars Pathfinder took 16,000 images of Mars. Some (*above*) showed the Sojourner rover at work.

Mars rover

Mars Pathfinder's rover was called Sojourner. It drove across the surface of the planet and went up close to many of the rocks near the Pathfinder to analyze them. Sojourner found volcanic rocks and rocks that had been eroded by wind.

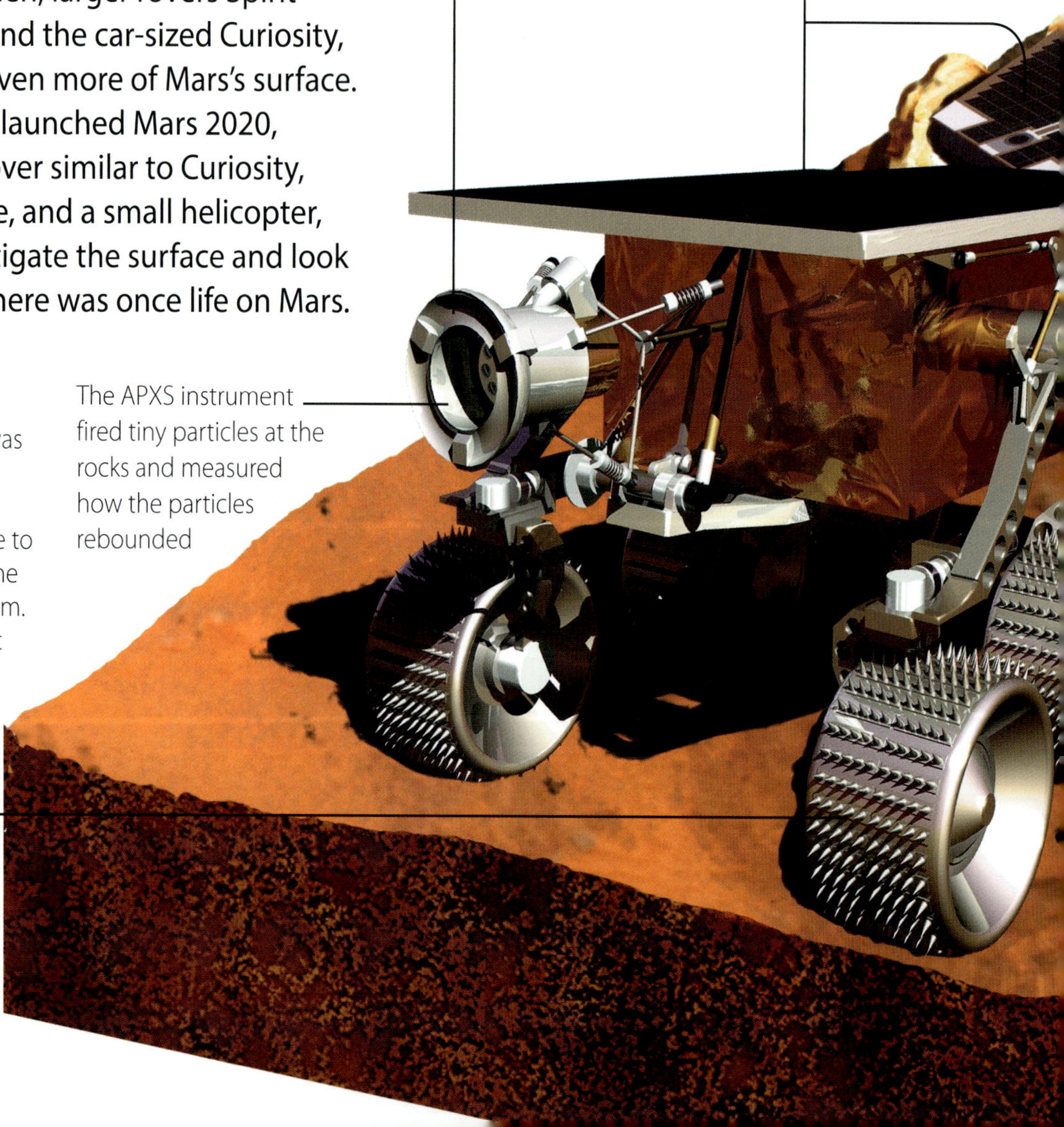

The rover analyzed 15 rocks in detail

Solar panels on Mars Pathfinder's petals and on top of Sojourner collected energy

The APXS instrument fired tiny particles at the rocks and measured how the particles rebounded

Sojourner's wheels had spikes to grip the soil

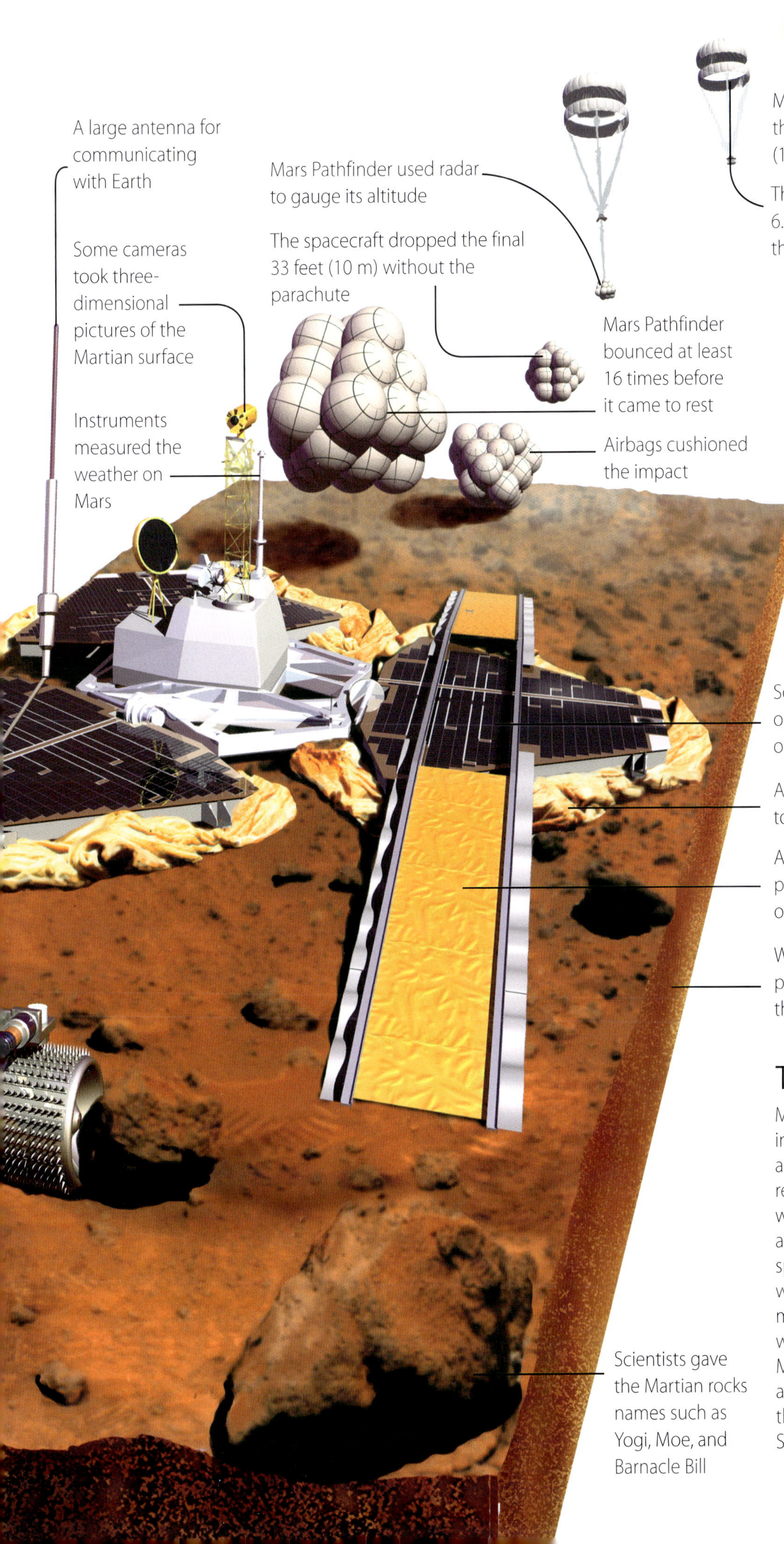

Landing on Mars

Instead of using bulky rockets to slow it down for landing, Mars Pathfinder was fitted with large airbags. These inflated as it neared the surface and prevented the lander from being damaged as it struck the rocky surface of Mars.

The Mars lander

Mars Pathfinder was split into two vehicles – a lander and a rover. The lander took readings of the Martian weather conditions, such as temperature and wind speed. It stayed in contact with Earth and it relayed messages to the rover. It was renamed the Sagan Memorial Station shortly after it landed in honor of the famous scientist Carl Sagan, who had just died.

Voyager

Two of the most ambitious space missions ever undertaken were those of the space probes Voyager 1 and 2. Voyager 2 was launched on August 20, 1977, and Voyager 1 a few weeks later on September 5, 1977. Voyager 1 followed a faster route to Jupiter and overtook Voyager 2 on the way.

In March 1979, Voyager 1 flew by Jupiter and transmitted scientific information and images of the planet to Earth. It continued on, flying by Saturn and its largest moon, Titan, in November 1980. Voyager 2 reached Jupiter in July and Saturn in 1981. Unlike Voyager 1, it did not fly close to Titan. Instead, it continued to Uranus. In January 1986, it transmitted pictures of that pale blue-green planet before continuing its journey onward to Neptune. In August 1989, Voyager 2 reached Neptune for the final flyby of its mission.

It was not until 2015 that the even more distant dwarf planet Pluto was visited by a probe, NASA's New Horizons spacecraft.

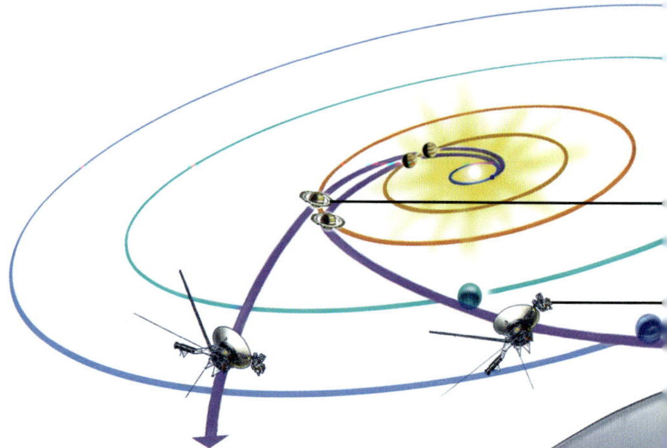

The grand tour

The Voyager space probes followed paths, or trajectories, that made use of gravity assists. These trajectories were first worked out in 1965 by Gary Flandro, who realized that the four gas giants (*see page 10*) line up once every 175 years. This alignment meant that a probe could visit the gas giants in turn and use each planet's gravity to propel it onwards to the next. He calculated that they would next line up in the 1980s, and so the idea for the Voyager missions was born.

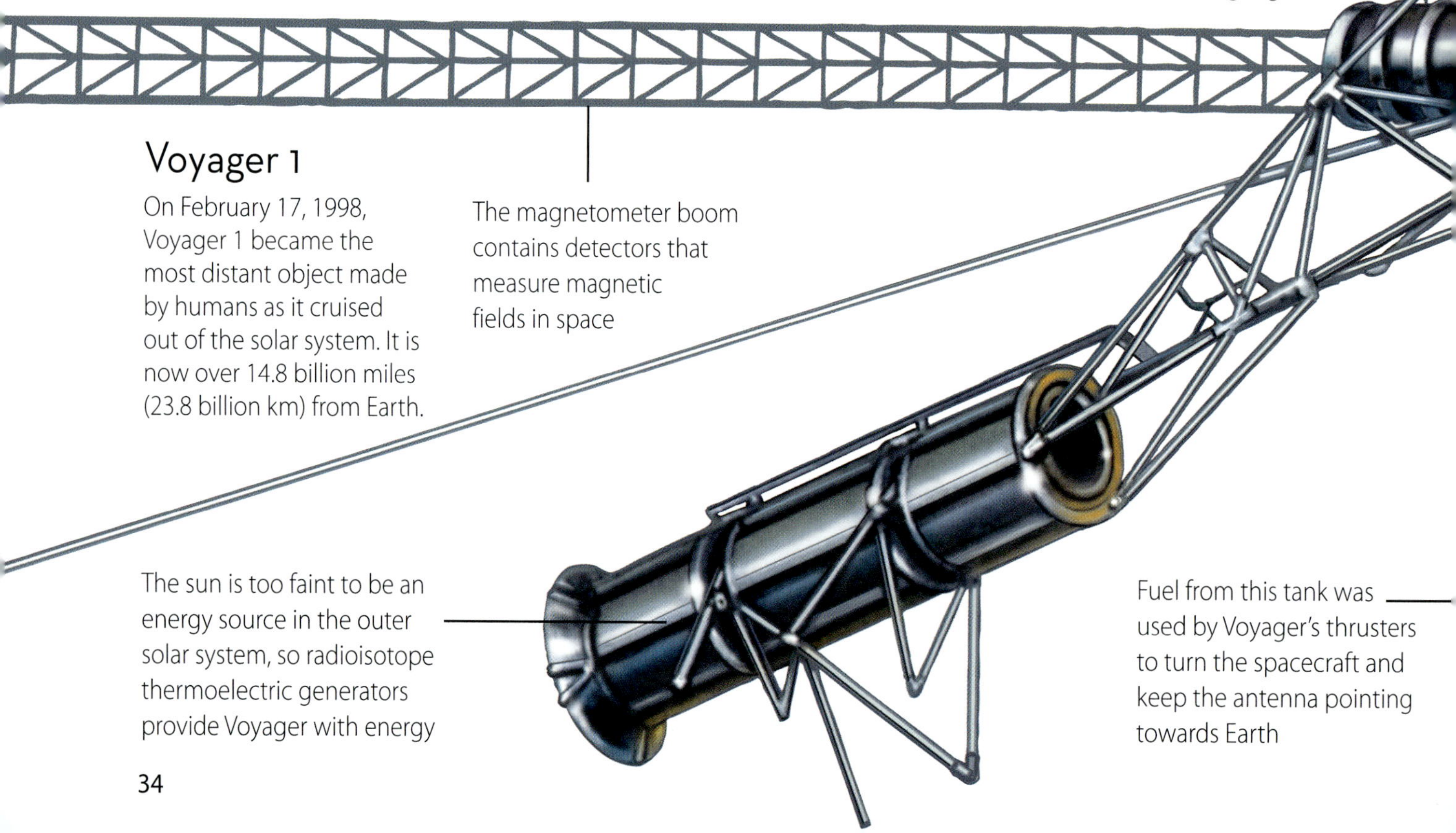

Voyager 1

On February 17, 1998, Voyager 1 became the most distant object made by humans as it cruised out of the solar system. It is now over 14.8 billion miles (23.8 billion km) from Earth.

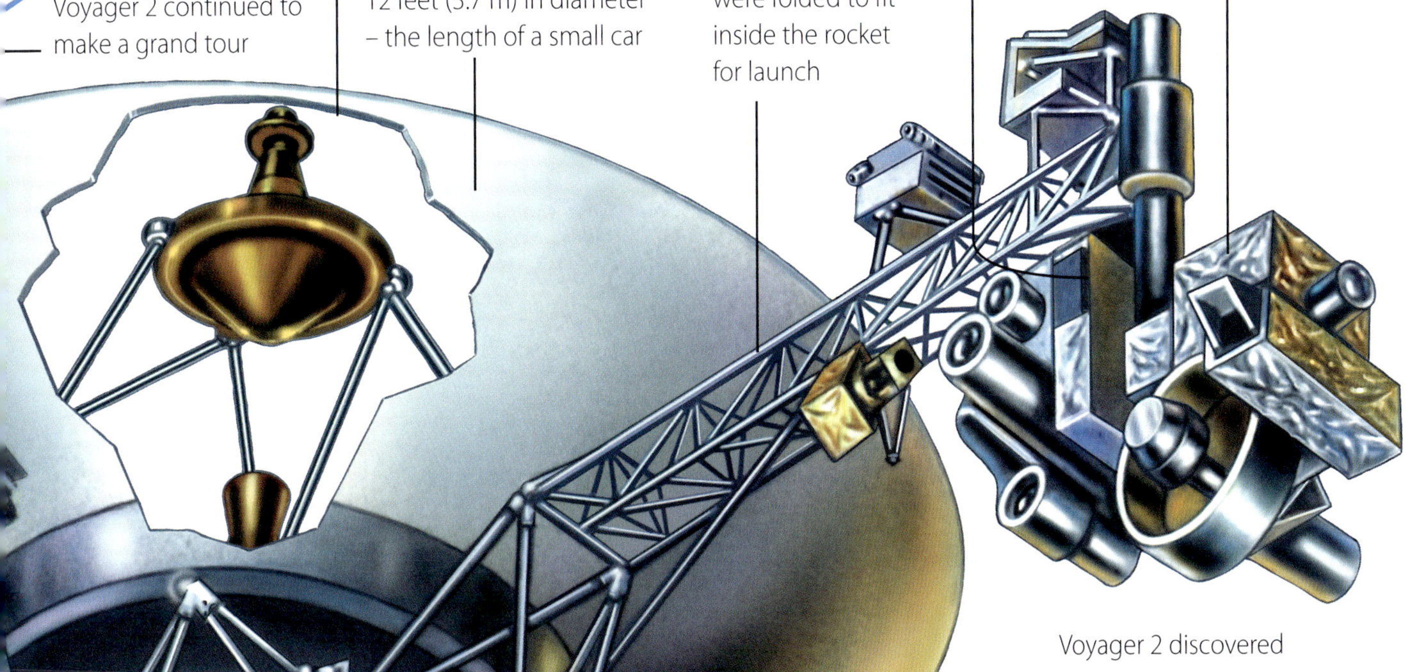
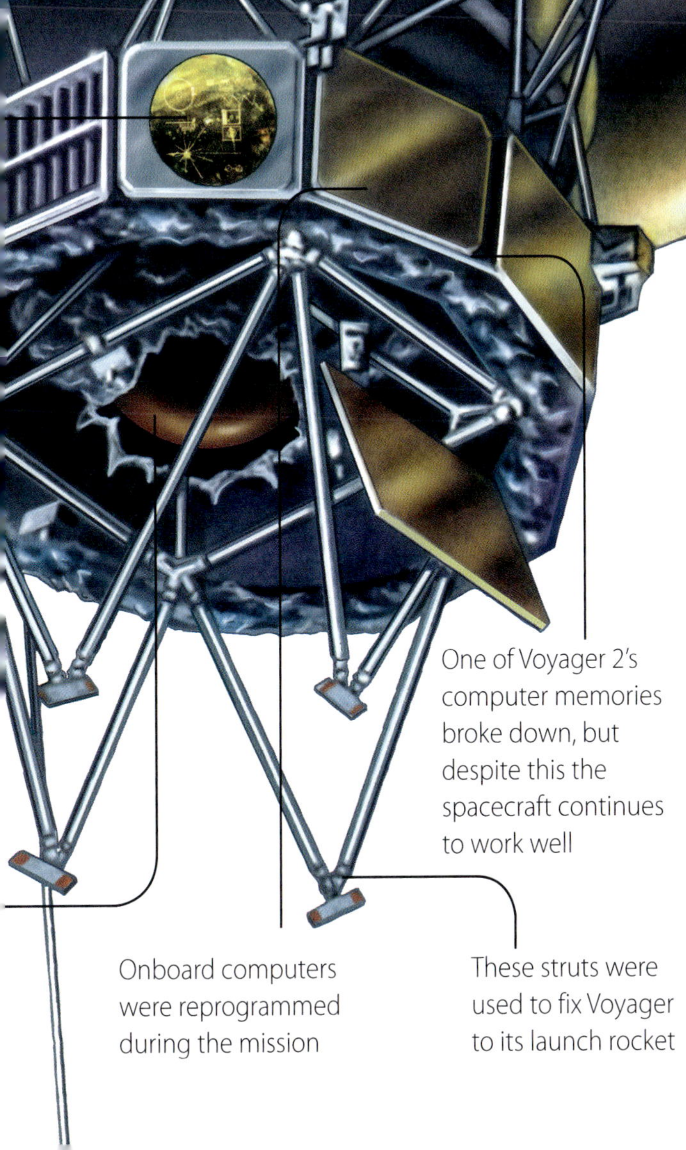

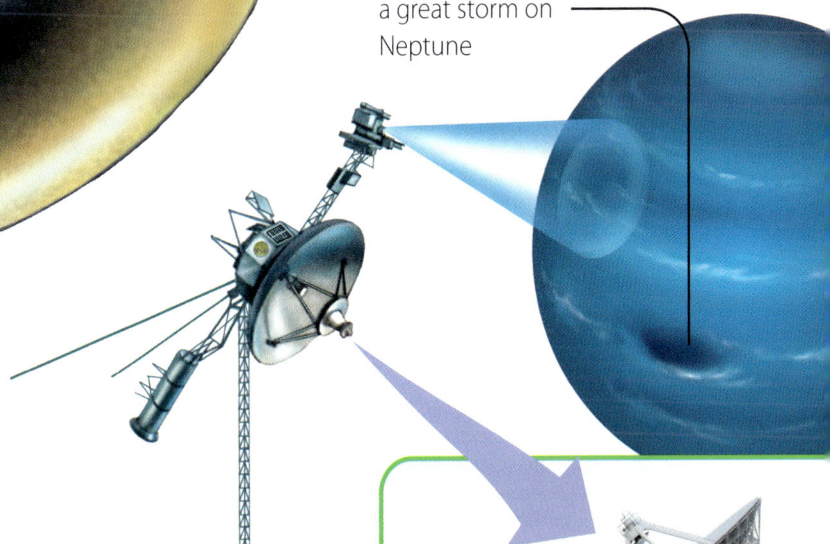

Pictures from space

The Voyager camera only transmitted black-and-white images, but computers could apply filters to create colored versions. If an object was too big for the camera to capture in a single image, many photographs were taken and then pieced together, again by computer.

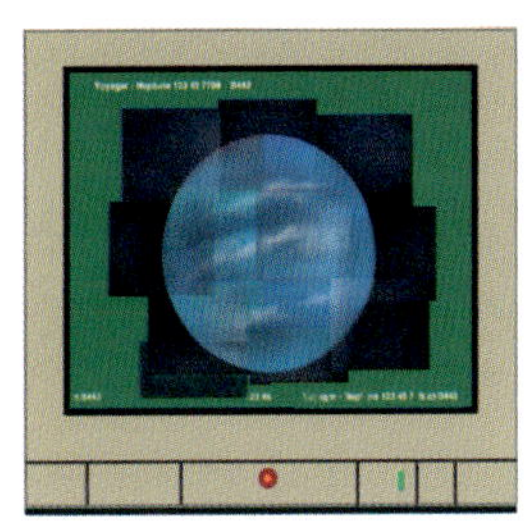

Studying the Stars

Astronomers use very large telescopes to study the universe. These telescopes have two mirrors that focus light and are kept in observatories (*right*). Like any piece of machinery, a telescope sometimes needs to be repaired, so everything that is necessary to keep it working is found in an observatory.

Using computer-controlled motors, the telescope operator sitting in the control room can move the telescope. Another astronomer working alongside collects data. A range of cameras and other instruments, known as detectors, can be found at an observatory. Astronomers use them to record their observations by attaching them to the base of the telescope inside a metal cage. Data is fed to the control room and images are then processed and displayed on a computer screen. The images can then be analyzed by other astronomers around the world.

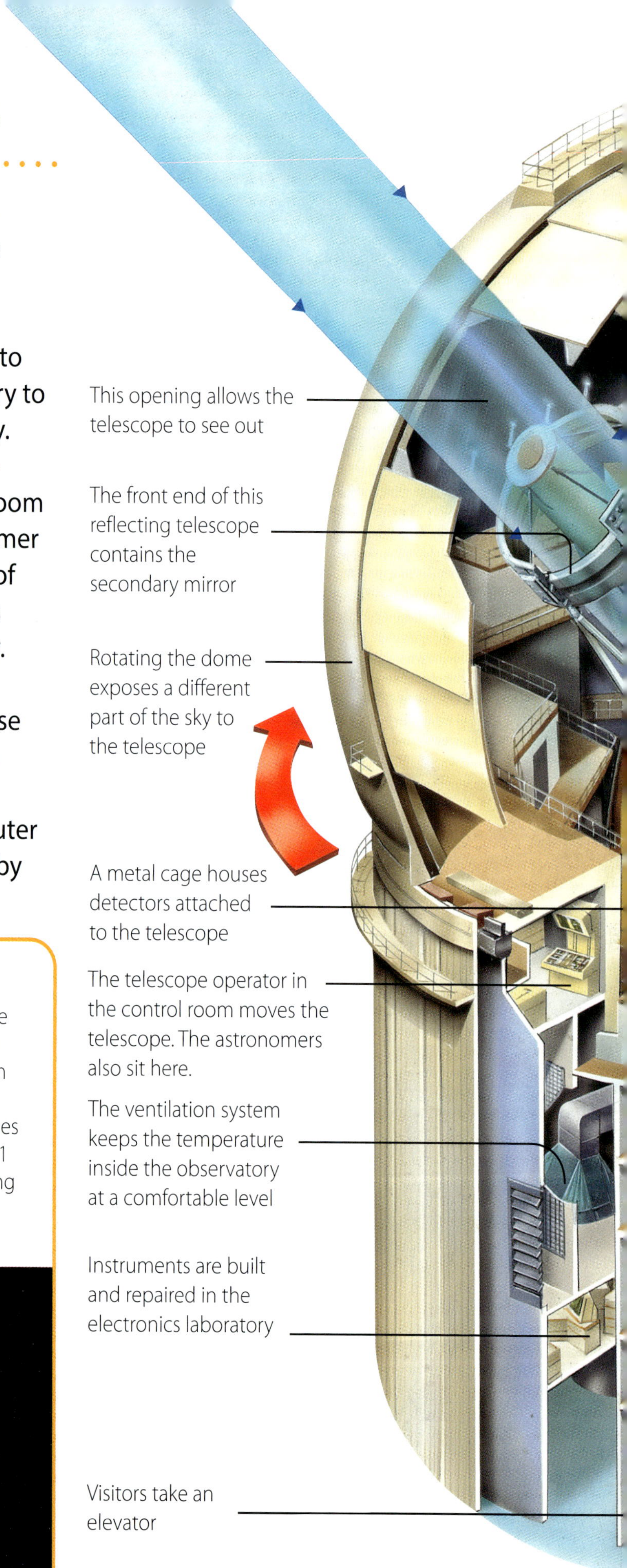

Space telescopes

Placing telescopes in outer space avoids interference from Earth's atmosphere and allows astronomers to study the universe in ways that are not possible from the ground. Space telescopes can "see"gamma rays, ultraviolet and infrared light, or even X-rays. The James Webb Space Telescope (*below*) was launched in 2021 and is the largest optical telescope in space. It is using infrared light to find some of the oldest and faintest galaxies formed after the Big Bang (*see pages 6–7*).

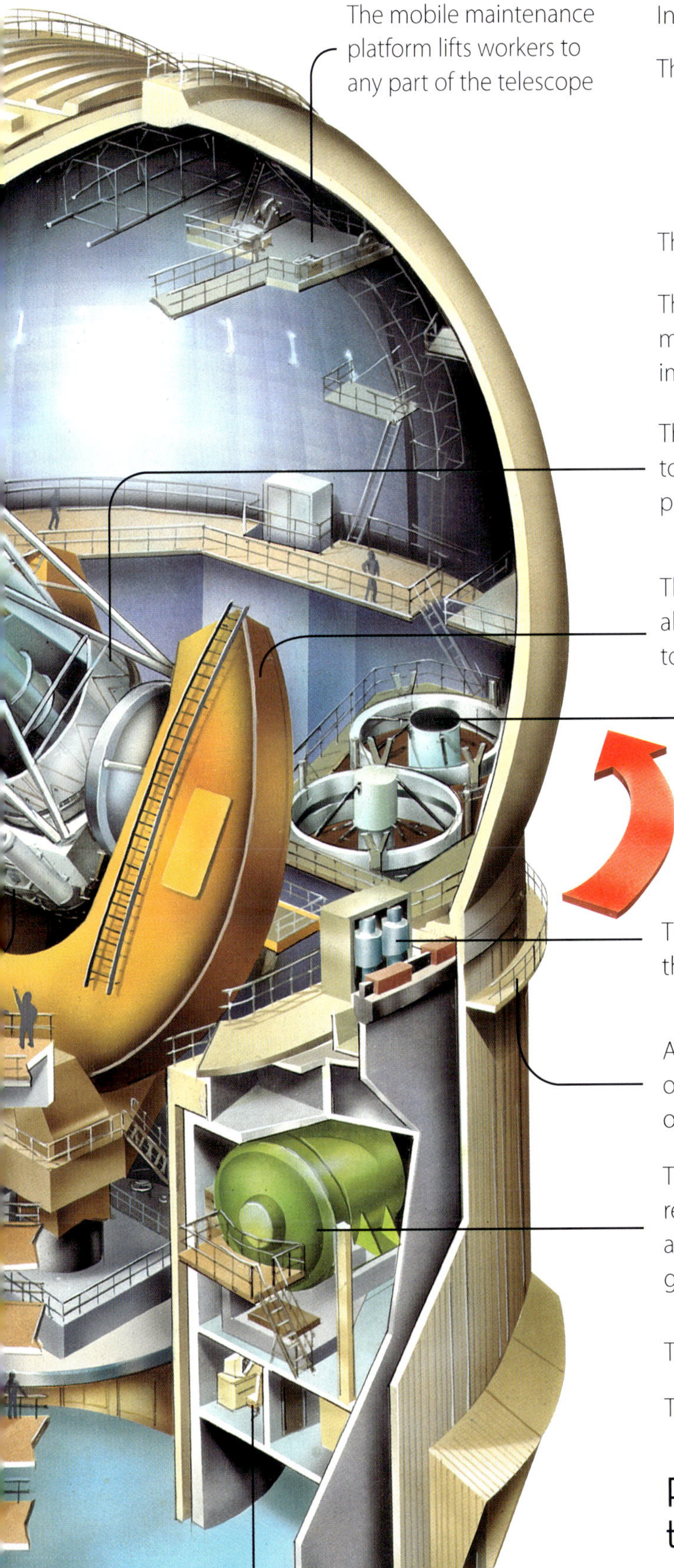

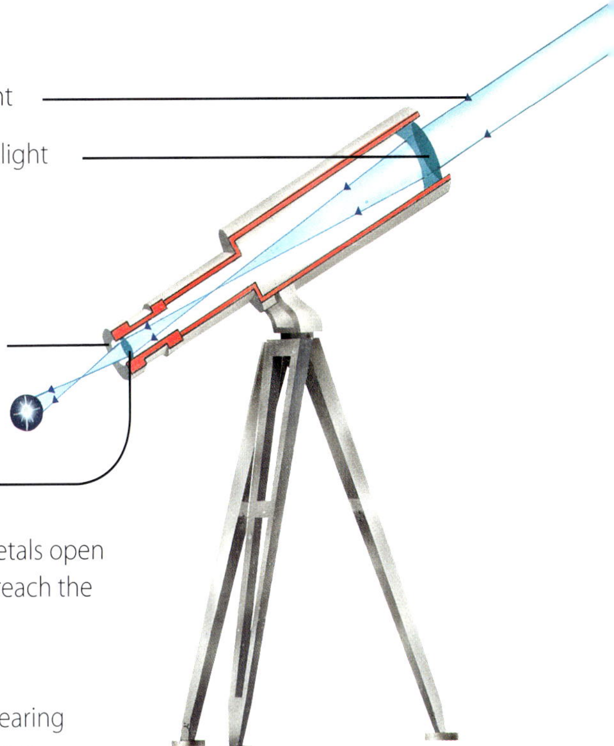

Refracting telescope

A refracting telescope brings light to a focus by using two lenses. The first is known as the objective lens and focuses the light just before the eyepiece. The eyepiece lens then magnifies the image so the observer can see it comfortably.

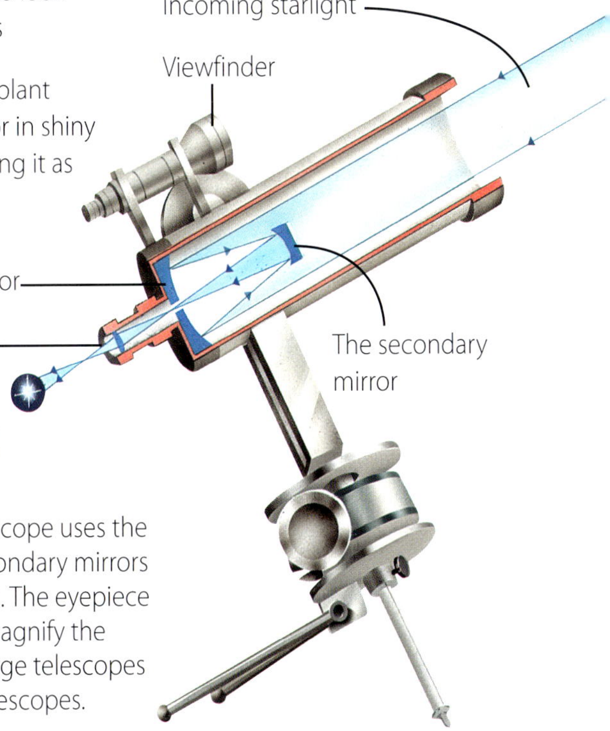

Reflecting telescope

A reflecting telescope uses the primary and secondary mirrors to focus starlight. The eyepiece lens is used to magnify the image. All the large telescopes are reflecting telescopes.

Stars

Stars are enormous energy generators. They are born in collapsing clouds of hydrogen gas. The gas is squeezed so tightly that its temperature rises. When the temperature in the center of the star reaches 18 million °F (10 million °C), the hydrogen atoms' nuclei collide with such force that they fuse (stick together) and form new nuclei. This nuclear fusion leads to the formation of helium nuclei and the release of energy that makes the star shine.

Stars come in many sizes. The sun is a little bigger than most other stars, but some stars have a hundred times the mass of the sun. Stars that contain the most mass do not live as long as stars with little mass. A very high-mass star will only live a few million years, while a low-mass star, such as the sun, could last nine billion years or more.

The corona

The outermost gas around the sun is called the corona. It spreads out very thinly through space and usually cannot be seen because the photosphere of the sun is so bright. During a solar eclipse, the moon blocks out the light from the photosphere and the dimmer corona can be seen around the edge.

The life of a star

At the first stage of a star's life, the star is the center of a collapsing gas cloud (1). When the core of a protostar is hot enough, hydrogen begins to fuse and the protostar becomes a star (2). For most of its life a star will generate

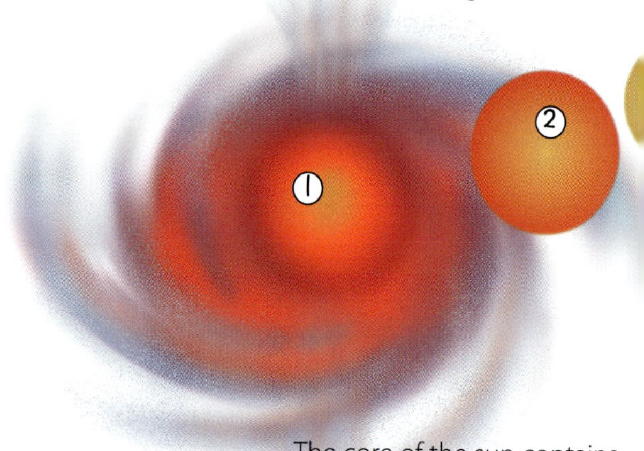

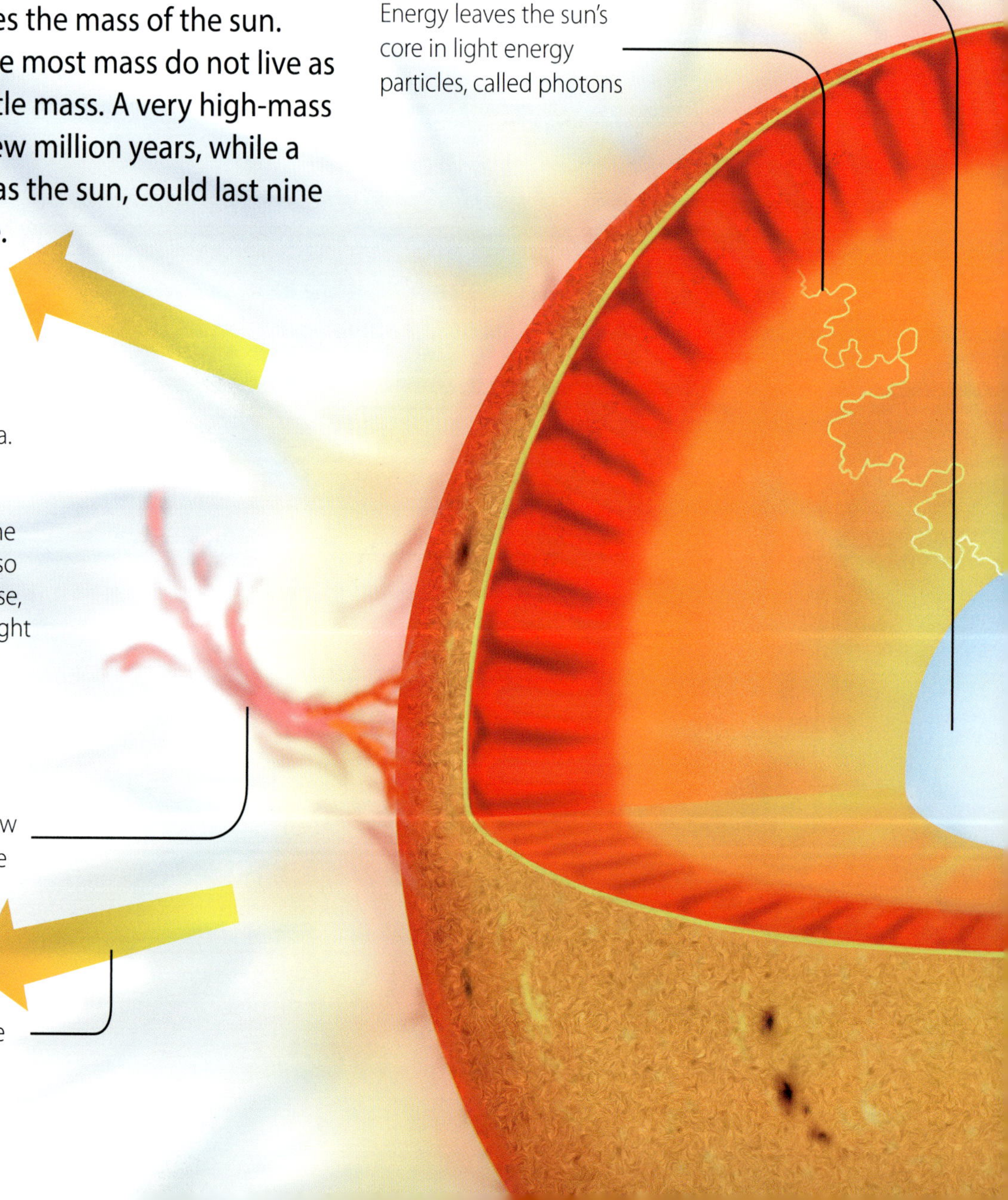

energy and change very little (3). As the star grows older it begins to increase in size and the amount of energy it generates (4). Late in the star's life it begins to pulsate (expand and contract) (5). Nuclear fusion takes place in bursts, rather than continuously. The unstable nuclear fusion in the star lifts its outer layers and throws them off into space. The result is known as a planetary nebula (6) because such an object looked like a planet to astronomers in the 1700s.

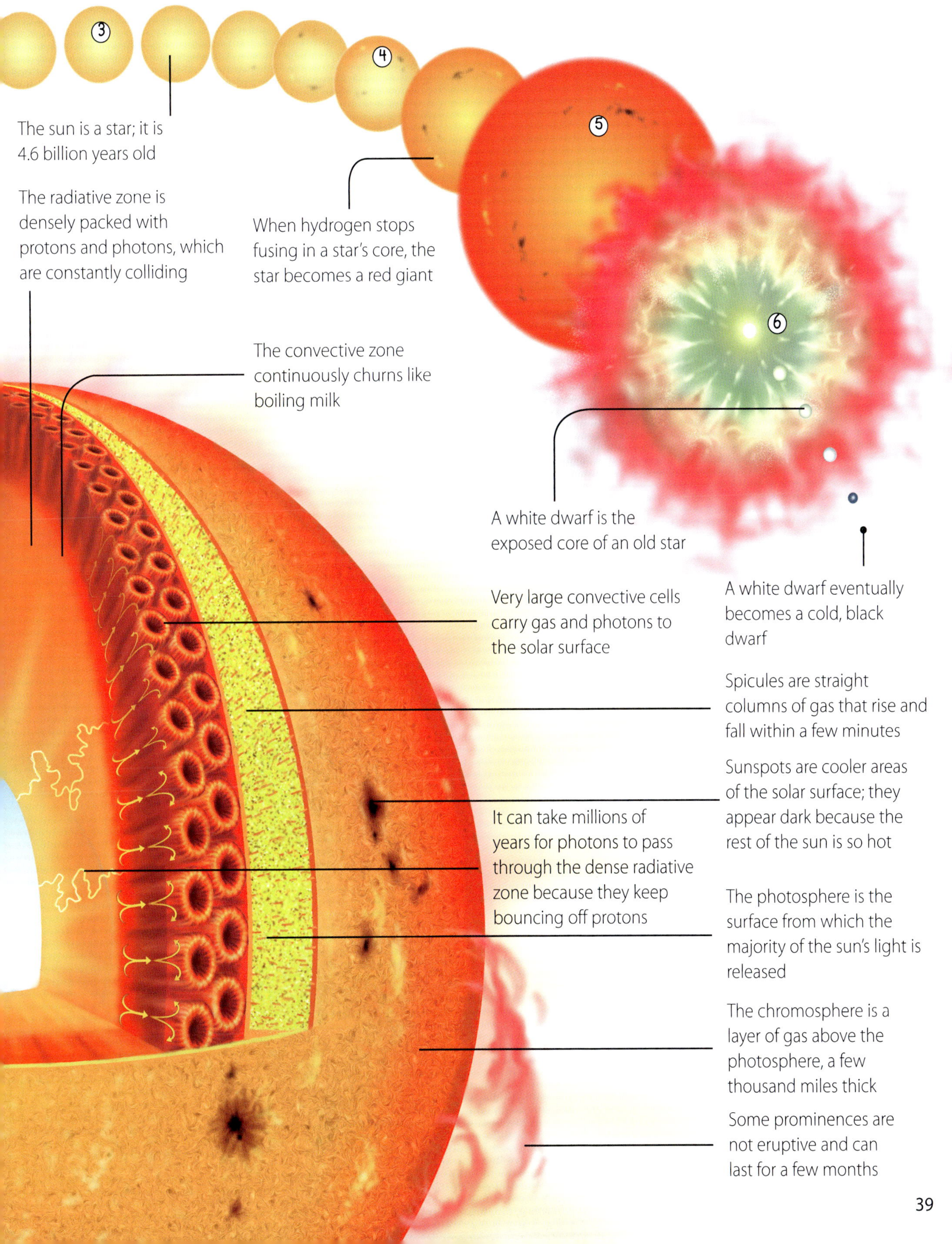

Black Holes

A black hole is one of the most remarkable objects in the universe. It is an incredibly dense object which possesses so much gravity that nothing can escape from it. Light is the fastest thing in the universe and yet not even light can escape from a black hole.

In order to escape the gravitational pull of Earth, a rocket must reach a speed of about 7 miles (11.2 km) per second. This is known as the escape velocity. If the Earth were squeezed into a smaller volume, making it more dense, its gravitational pull would be greater and the escape velocity would increase. If the Earth were squeezed to the size of a marble, the escape velocity would go up so much that it would be equal to the speed of light – 186,000 miles (300,000 km) per second. At this point, nothing would escape its gravitational pull and the Earth would become a black hole.

Patches of radio waves at the ends of jets are known as radio lobes

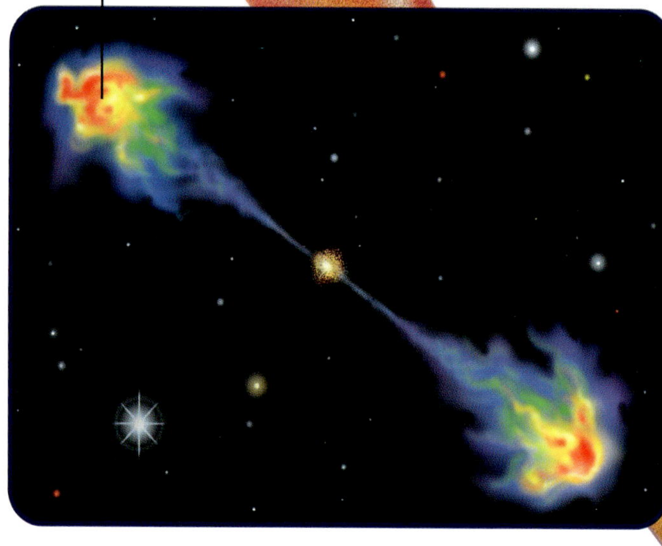

Active galaxies

Some galaxies contain supermassive black holes. These are called active galaxies. Sometimes, jets shoot out from the core, far into space. The particles collide with each other and produce radio waves which can be picked up by radio telescopes. In the picture above, the radio waves have been color-coded by a computer. Only some active galaxies produce radio waves – it is not yet known why.

The torus is a large disk of dust and gas surrounding a supermassive black hole

The torus is often surrounded by clouds of gas that are turning into stars

Stellar black holes

A stellar black hole is created when a massive star explodes. For example, a black hole (1) can be created when a massive star in a binary (double) star system explodes. The second star (2) is pulled to pieces and swallowed by the black hole. As it orbits the black hole, gas streams from the star onto a disk around the black hole before being consumed. The gas becomes so hot that it gives off X-rays – these can be detected by X-ray telescopes. This is how the black hole Cygnus X-1 was created.

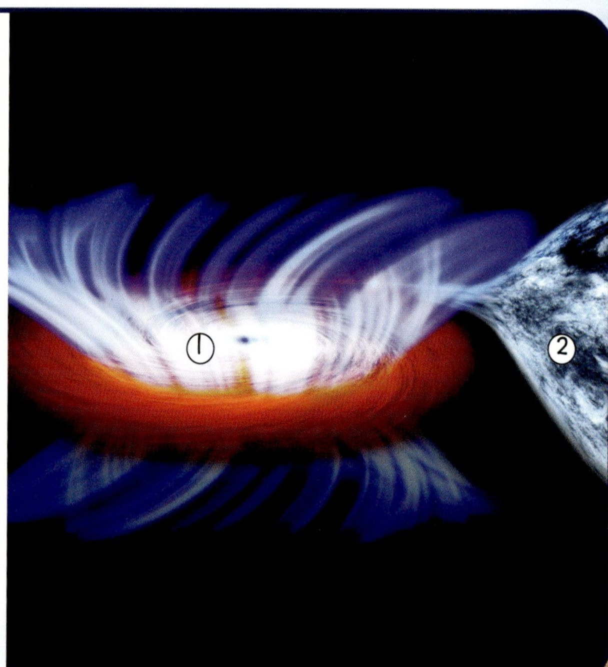

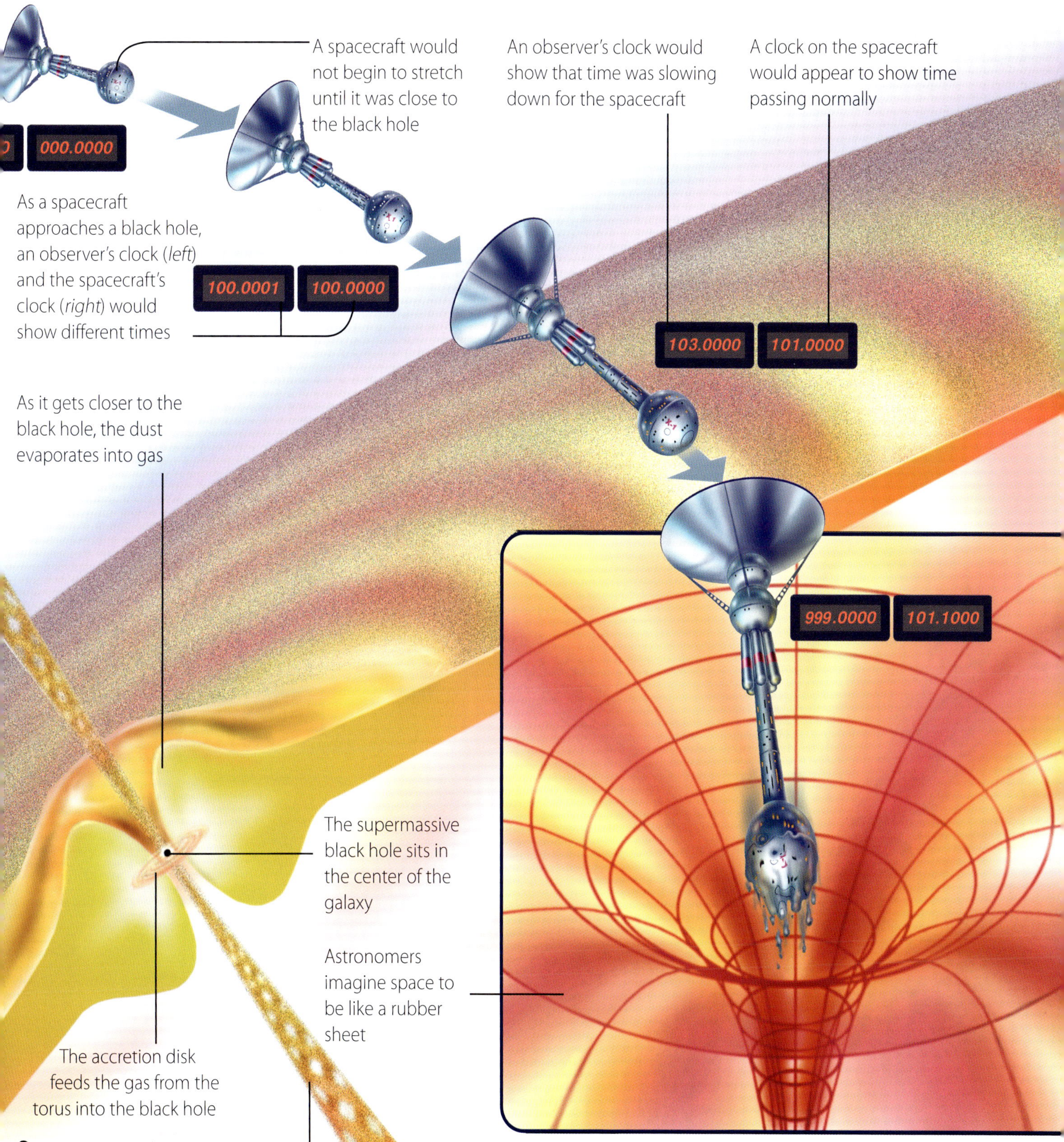

Supermassive black holes

The supermassive black hole is at the center of an active galaxy (*above*). This is millions of times more massive than a stellar black hole. It is produced when matter falls together to form the galaxy.

Falling into a black hole

If a spacecraft were to fall into a black hole, it would be destroyed. As the spacecraft got closer, the gravitational force would strengthen. The end closest to the black hole would be pulled more, stretching the craft until it was pulled to bits. Time passes more slowly near an object with gravity, such as a black hole, so a distant observer would see time slowing down for the craft as it got closer to the black hole. On the spacecraft, time would appear to pass normally.

Radio Telescopes

For centuries, telescopes have collected light and focused it into images. However, light is not the only type of radiation released by objects in space. Many also give out radio waves. In order to collect radio waves a special telescope, called a radio telescope, is needed. Radio telescopes are very large dishes which collect radio waves and focus them onto a small detector in the center of the dish.

The study of radio waves from space has given astronomers new ideas about galaxies. In particular, they have learned that some active galaxies are powerful emitters of radio waves (*see page 40*). Some astronomers also use radio telescopes to search for messages from space. They are trying to find other life in the universe, which may communicate using radio waves. No messages have been received so far.

The Effelsberg Radio Telescope

The Effelsberg Radio Telescope has a collecting dish with an area of 84,500 square feet (7,850 sq. m). It collects radio waves with this dish and focuses them onto three detectors. The three detectors collect radio waves from three slightly different parts of the sky and this speeds up the process of building an image.

Radio images from space

Radio waves picked up by the radio telescope's detectors are combined into a single image. Different radio intensities are color-coded. To obtain higher-quality images, several radio telescopes can be used together. Two or more radio telescopes observe the same object at the same time. The signals received by each telescope can then be compared and used to form detailed pictures.

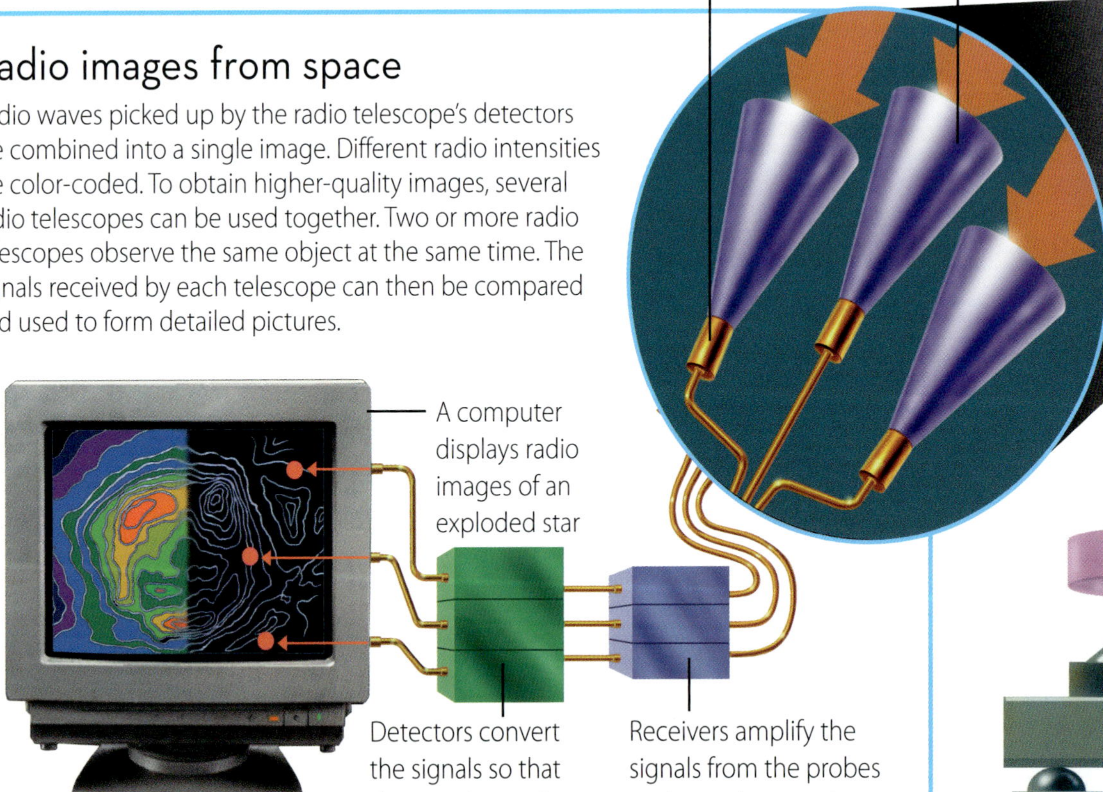

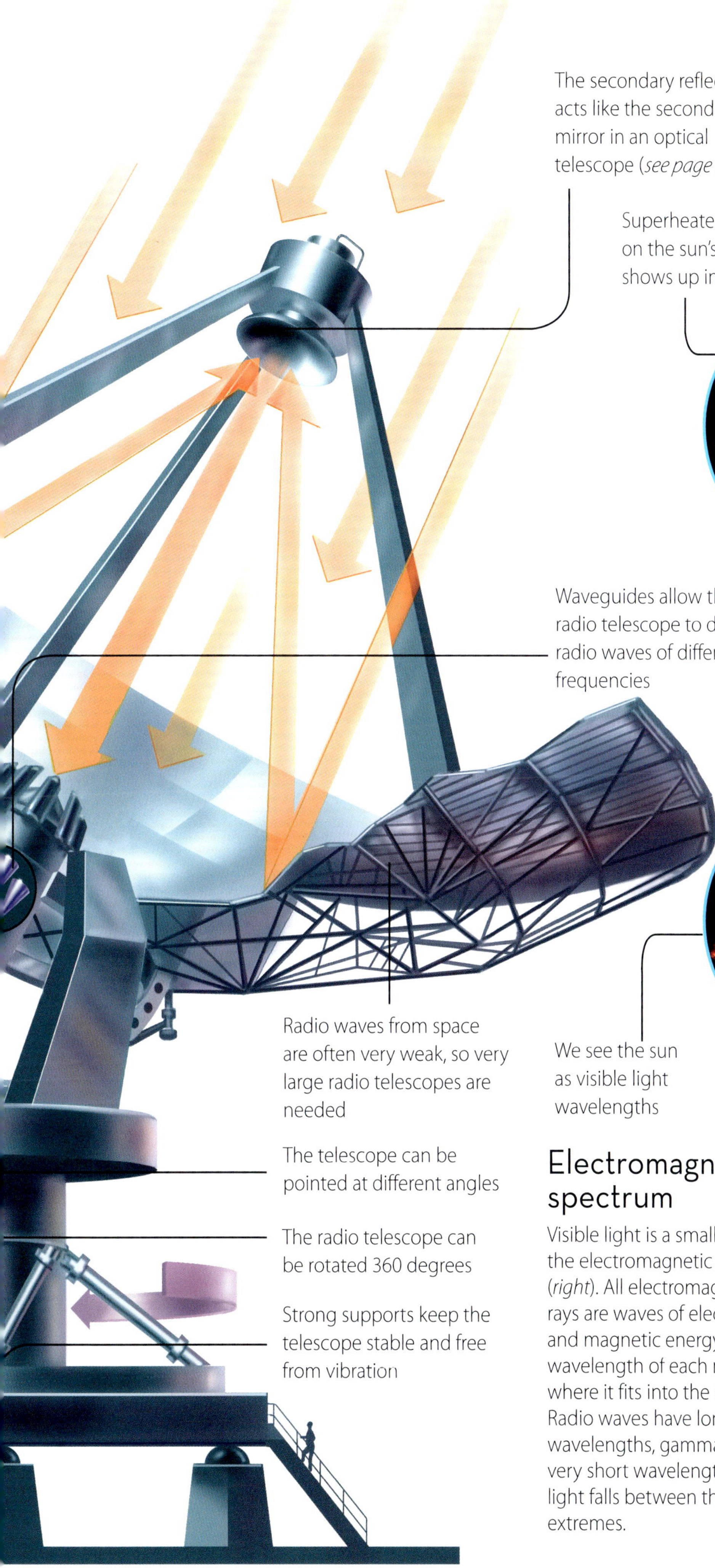

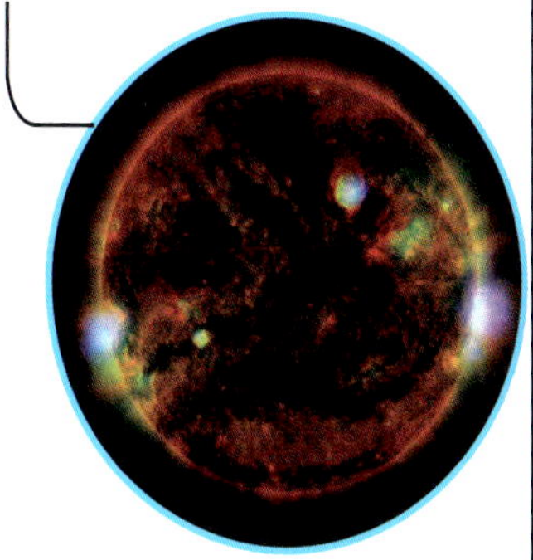

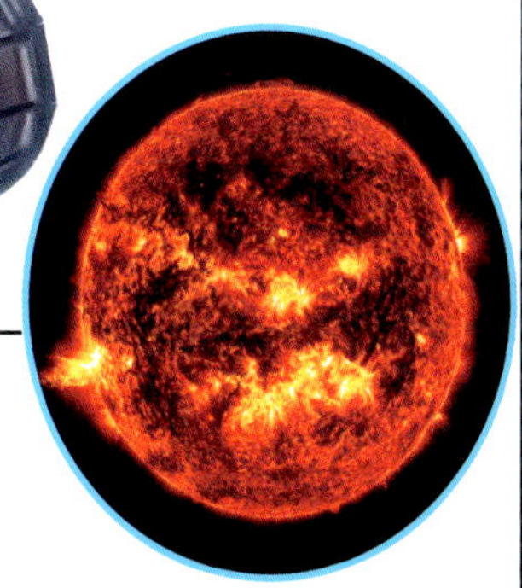

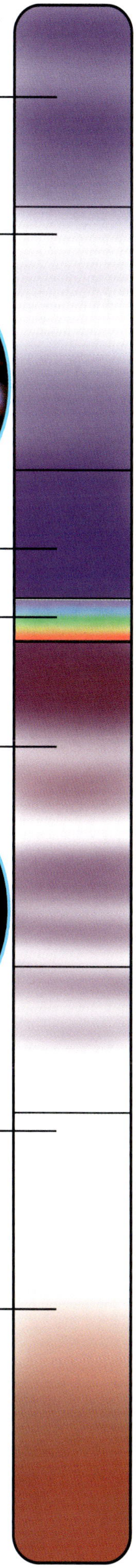

Electromagnetic spectrum

Visible light is a small part of the electromagnetic spectrum (*right*). All electromagnetic rays are waves of electric and magnetic energy. The wavelength of each ray decides where it fits into the spectrum. Radio waves have long wavelengths, gamma rays have very short wavelengths. Visible light falls between the two extremes.

Magnetic Fields

A magnetic field is generated every time an electrically charged object moves. Most of the planets in the solar system are known to generate magnetic fields. Earth's magnetic field is generated in its fluid, outer core. This is because the heat of the inner core drives the fluid in the outer core up and around in a process called convection. Because this outer core is made of metal, which can be electrically charged, the convection causes a magnetic field to be generated.

The planets Mercury, Venus, and Mars generate their magnetic fields in similar ways, but compared to Earth's, their fields are very weak. In the center of Jupiter and Saturn, hydrogen gas is compressed to behave like a metal and this generates magnetic fields. In Uranus and Neptune, the generating material is thought to be ice.

Magnetic poles

All of the magnetic fields behave as if a gigantic bar magnet were buried in the center of the planet. Invisible lines of magnetic force come out through the magnetic north pole of the planet and back in through the magnetic south pole. (The magnetic poles are the opposite of the geographic poles.)

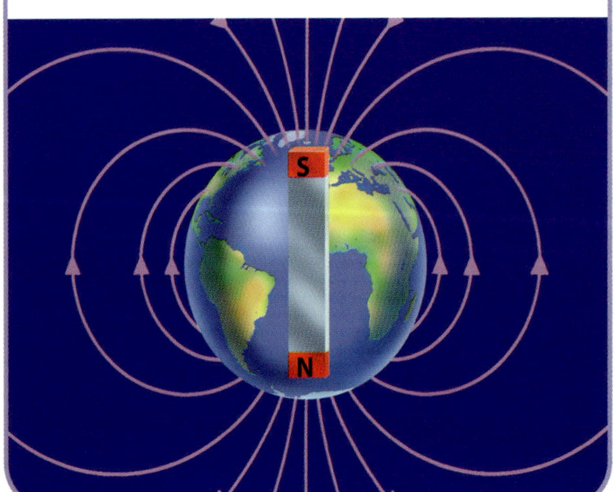

Auroral display

Tiny particles carrying electrical charges are continuously streaming away from the sun. Sometimes these get caught in Earth's magnetic field and are drawn into the atmosphere near the North and South Poles. When these charged particles hit molecules in the atmosphere, they cause them to glow. This is known as an auroral display.

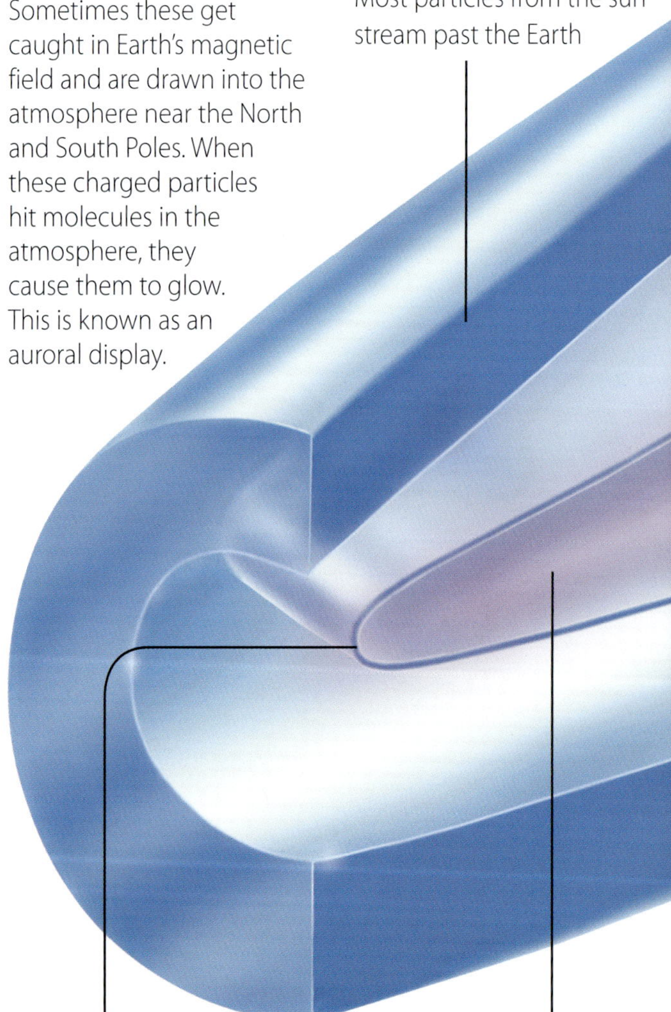

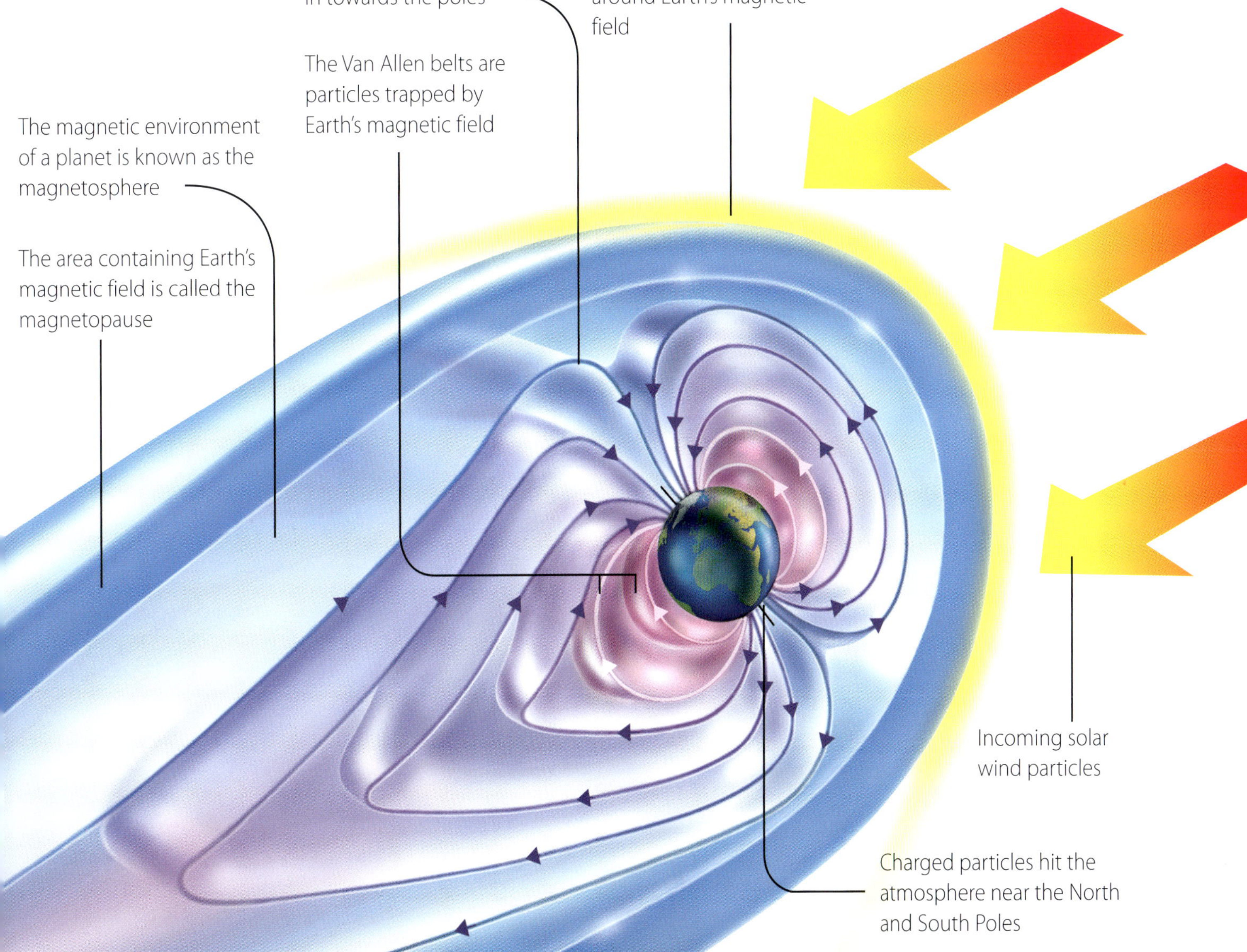

The solar wind

The sun continuously throws off tiny particles that carry an electrical charge. These particles are bits of atoms that are flung outwards from close to the sun's surface. As the sun spins it flings them off in a spiral pattern. The wind of particles blows around Earth's magnetosphere, pulling it out into a tail on the far side.

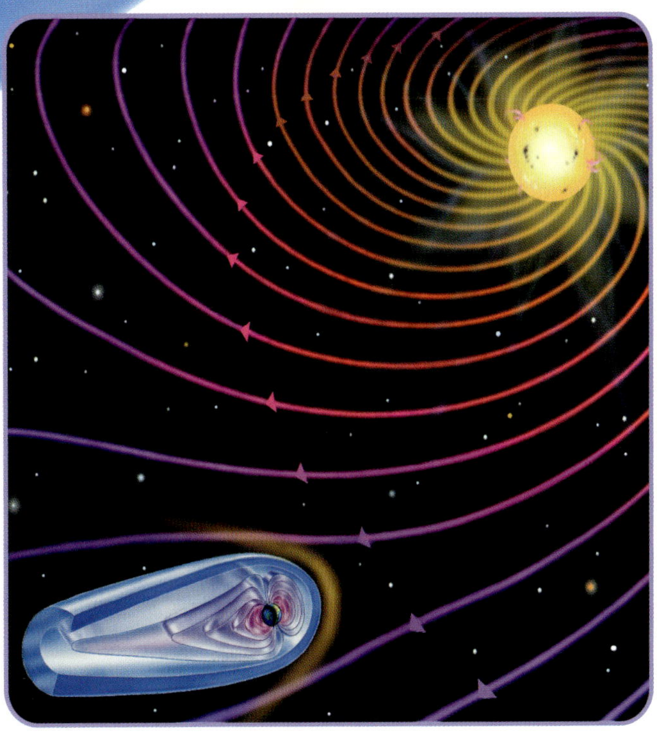

Index

A
Andromeda 8
Apollo missions 16, 20–23
Ariane rocket 17
Armstrong, Neil 20
asteroid belt 10, 11
astronauts 18, 20, 22–24, 26–29
atmosphere 15
attitude jets 26
auroral display 44

B
Big Bang 6–7
black holes 40–41

C
Cape Canaveral 24
celestial sphere 15
Charon 12
comets 14
command and service module 18
control box, spacesuit 27
corona 38

E
early missions 18–19
Earth 10, 11, 14–15
  magnetic field 44–45
  orbit 9, 14
Effelsberg Radio Telescope 42–43
ejection, astronaut 18–19
electromagnetic spectrum 43
elliptical orbit 9
emergency procedure 19
escape velocity 40
Europa 12
expanding universe 9

F
flight path 17
fuel tank 16, 17, 24

G
Gagarin, Yuri 18
galaxies 6–7, 8–9, 36
  active 40
  barred-spiral 8
  elliptical 8
  Milky Way 7, 8–9, 10
  spiral 8
Goddard, Robert 16
gravity 10

H
habitation module 28
Hubble, Edwin 9
Humason, Milton 9

I
instrument module 18
International Space Station 28–29
Io 12

J
James Webb Space Telescope 36
Jupiter 10–11, 12–13, 34, 44

L
landing
  on Earth 18–19, 21, 25
  on Mars 31–32
  module 20–21
  on moon 20–21, 22, 30
light-years 8
Lunar Prospector 22
lunar rock 23
lunar roving vehicle 22–23

M
magnetic fields 44–45
magnetic poles 44
manned moon missions 20
mantle (Earth's) 14
Mars 10, 12, 13, 44
  Global Surveyor 32
  landing on 31–33
  Pathfinder 32–33
  pictures of 31
  rover 32–33
  Viking lander 30–31
matter 6, 12
Mercury 10, 13, 44
Milky Way 7, 8–9, 10
Mir 28
moon (of Earth) 12
  missions to 16, 20–23
  orbit 9
  phases 11
moons of planets 12, 34, 35

N
Neptune 10, 11, 12, 34, 44
Newton, Sir Isaac 16

O
orbits 8, 9
  Earth 9, 14
  moon 9
  planets 10
  rockets and spacecraft 19, 20, 21

P
Pathfinder 32–33
payload 16
planets 8, 9, 12–13
  magnetic fields 44–45
  orbits 10
Pluto 10, 11, 12
Portable Life Support System (PLSS)
  22

Q
quarks 6

R
radio telescopes 42–43
redshift 9
rings 10, 12
robotic arm 31
rocket fuel 16, 17
rockets and spacecraft 16–17
  Apollo 16, 20–23
  in black hole 41
  flight profile 18
  orbits 19, 20, 21
  Space Shuttle 16, 24–25, 29
  space stations 28–29
  Vostok 18–19
  Voyager 34–35
rocks 23, 31, 33
rotation, Earth 15

S
Salyut 28
satellites 16, 24–25
Saturn 10, 11, 12, 13, 35, 44
Saturn V (rocket) 16
science modules 29
seasons 14
Skylab 28
Sojourner 32–33
solar system 7, 9, 10–11
solar wind 45
Soyuz 16, 28
space probes 22, 34–35
Space Shuttle 16, 24–25, 29
space stations 28–29
spacesuit 26–27
space telescopes 36
spacewalking 26–27
stars 15, 36–37, 38–39
sun 8, 10, 11, 38–39
sunspots 39
superclusters 8
surveyor probes 22, 23

T
telescopes 36–37, 42–43
Tereshkova, Valentina 18
Titan 12, 34, 35

U
universe 8–9
Uranus 10, 12, 44

V
Venus 10, 13, 44
Viking landers 30–31
Vostok 18–19
Voyager 34–35